YVONNE BAILEY'S

BOOK OF SYMBOLS

AND DREAMS

First published in Great Britain by
Spiritworldonline Ltd
9 Barquentine Place
Atlantic Wharf
Cardiff
CF10 4NF

http://www.spiritworldonline.com

A CIP record for this book is available from the British Library.

ISBN 0-9550612-1-0

Printed and bound in Great Britain by Creative Print and Design Wales, Ebbw Vale.

Yvonne has also written a booked entitled 'The Making of a Spiritual Medium'.

A brief description of that book is as follows:

'The Making of a Spiritual Medium is a book about spirit communication and personal growth. It is written to help those who are walking the spiritual path. More importantly, it should be of immense help to those who are being dragged, kicking and screaming along the path. It is an example of a spiritual journey.

The pages tell of growing up in Cardiff, Wales in the UK in the 1950/1960s and the hardships and frailties of the working class people. The flavour of the exotic docklands area known as Tiger Bay is brilliantly brought to life. Interwoven through the story are the spiritual experiences that happened to the author from a small child, and her eventual search for answers. The book should answer some of the mysteries of life such as coincidence, telepathy, dreams and sleep paralysis and it truly is compelling reading'.

Yvonne has written 'The Making of a Spiritual Medium', and this book of symbols and dreams, to give the reader a complete understanding of spirit communication. It is highly recommended that both books be read for the reader to gain maximum benefit.

You can order the books or contact Yvonne by visiting http://www.spiritworldonline.com or writing to:

Spiritworldonline Ltd.,
9 Barquentine Place
Atlantic Wharf
Cardiff
CF10 4NF

Grateful thanks to Joyce, for introducing me to the universal language of symbols.

I would also like to give thanks to the many people who have shared their dreams and symbolic happenings with me.

Without all of your input this book could not have been written.

Yve xx

CONTENTS :

1   Dreams, symbolic
happenings
and their meanings.   1 – 74

2   A – Z of symbols
and their meaning.   75 - 196

ONE

DREAMS,

SYMBOLIC HAPPENINGS

AND THEIR MEANINGS

I dreamt I was elevated and looking down on a wide open space. I noticed there were three cream coloured, seasoned leather chairs just sat out in the open. There was some kind of covering over them, perhaps like the kind of slatted wooden covering you get over a patio area. This seemed so out of place in this wide open space.

I say it was a dream but I am not sure as the images were so powerful and vivid to me.

There is a situation in your life that should be out in the open but three people in the family are sitting on something that is covered up. These people are 'the top', they are the cream and they are seasoned. In other words they have a lot of experience in this type of a cover up.

As the dream was so powerful you need to take notice as it is there for guidance.

Thank you so much for this interpretation. My daughter has gone missing and I am frantic to know where she is. She has gone missing before and I later found out she was staying with family members.

I am so upset as my boyfriend of eleven years has left me for another woman. He has been seeing her for two years without me knowing. I found out by accident and when I confronted him he refused to acknowledge he had done anything wrong. I have not been sleeping properly but when I eventually fall to sleep I have the same, vivid dream.

I am in a market place, wandering from stall to stall. Everything on sale seems cheap and tacky and the stallholders are trying to get me to buy, but I shake my head and walk away. The floor is strewn with rubbish and is uneven. As I am leaving a woman is entering and we look at one and other as we pass by.

Your boyfriend is the market place and what he has to offer is cheap and tacky. What is underfoot is rubbish and you are not buying it any more. The woman is the new lady coming in to his life.

Be grateful that you are now able to walk away and comfort yourself with the knowledge that what he has to offer will be of no value to this new woman.

In my dream I was very aware that I didn't like the dress I was wearing. It was blue, very long and completely covered me. This somehow seemed inappropriate. I looked out of the front window and a traffic warden was about to write a ticket for my car, which was also blue. I felt resigned.

There is something you are wearing (putting up with) in life that's making you feel blue. You have an inner knowing that to feel this way is misplaced or inappropriate.

Symbolically we are all cars and the traffic warden was letting you know you have parked too long in this situation and you need to move on. You know this and, in fact, are resigned to it. You need to find some inner strength to make the changes necessary.

It is true that I am suffering from depression and I know I have the power to change things by exercising and eating healthier, but it seems such an effort to do this and it is far easier just to sit in front of the television feeling miserable.

I had a dream I was in a hot air balloon and I was going up and up in the air. The balloon was a dark green and I was frightened because I was going too high. I was on my own and out of control.

I had a pair of sunglasses on and they were tinted red and I was irritated by them as they were stopping me seeing clearly. However, I was powerless to take them off and powerless to stop the balloon from going higher.

You are up in the air about something, talking a lot of hot air. The dark green tells me there is a lot of negativity around you and your way of thinking is out of control. Perhaps you are the only one that sees things in the way you see them? You are seeing red and cannot change your view of things. This is making you feel powerless and you need to lighten up and be more positive.

You can change your view by taking the blinkers off and balancing your emotions. Only you can do this and you need to put a lot of effort into changing, then you won't feel so isolated.

I dreamt I was sitting around a camp fire with two other people and one of the people threw a bucket of water on the fire and put it out. It was such a relief as the fire was burning me.

A camp fire is representative of emotions that are out in the open. Are there two people around you who you have a situation or issues with? One of them will act as a peace maker and is putting the fire out.

Once the fire is out you should leave things there because otherwise you will get burnt.

That is amazing. I do have a situation with someone and another person has offered to listen to my story so that they can try to help me. I have been a bit distrustful of this person and so far have not let him help.

I think I will now tell him what has happened so that he can hopefully put an end to this situation.

I had a dream last night and it has disturbed me. It's a bit vague, but I went in to a house and found lots of animals, particularly dogs. They were abandoned and, although not emaciated, they were hungry.

I set about looking for food to feed the animals, and I also gave them water. I was upset and a woman neighbour called with her young daughter. She was complaining about people leaving animals like this.

The house is you and you seem the type of person who collects waifs and strays, particularly men, as animals are people and dogs are men.   You are an easy touch, and even though these people are not starving, you still have the desire to feed them. Food can be representative of words and really you are wasting your time and energy on them. You are giving them water, which is giving them your life, as water is life.

The neighbour and her young daughter is that part of you which you are attached too, and allows people to play on your sympathy.

It's a part of you that hasn't grown, and it will do you no good to continue living this way. You need to toughen up.

It is true; I never seem to focus on me any more as I have so many people around me who have problems.

Every man who comes in to my life always has lots of issues and, off I go again, sorting his problems out. The relationships never work and I am really going to make an effort to be different from now on.

My father has died aged 92. He was sometimes abusive to me as a child and his actions played a significant part in a metal breakdown I suffered.

Lately I've been dreaming of him and I feel he is continuing to abuse me by returning to haunt me. In the dream I'm in a concrete room with a pit in the floor and a large slab partly covering it. My father is lying within like an unwrapped mummy, emaciated with his mouth gaping and teeth exposed. On the wall there's a coat of arms involving the head of a lion and crossed swords.

The room is your mind; your father is deep in the pit of it. You are letting your father continue to abuse you by preserving him and his ugly words.

The fact that he appears emaciated shows he should have no weight (influence) any more. The lion represents strength and you have the strength to leave this behind as the crossed swords symbolises the fight should be over.

In my dream I was living in the country. I had put my washing to dry in the bushes of the country lane leading to my house. I was in the lane collecting my washing, having left the door of my house open.

When I got back to the house with my arms full of washing, I was shocked to see a man was inside. I asked him what he was doing in my house and he said, 'you left the door open'.

I felt really vulnerable and did not like his arrogant air. He was acting as though he had a right to be there.

Stop airing your dirty washing for all to see. You are leaving yourself open to abuse by others, and not setting boundaries. They will not respect your privacy and this will leave you vulnerable.

You need to be careful when sharing your personal life with others as they could take advantage.

I dreamt I was in a room with my sister and there was murder going on, people were shouting and angry. The room had a window with red blood all over it. There was another sister with us, but I didn't recognize her. I could hear the thoughts of this sister and she was going to slash my knees to stop me from getting away.

Next this sister was out in the garden putting her underwear out to dry. I was pretending that all was okay.

You are in a volatile situation and there is murder going on. A window is our view on life and your view is emotionally imbalanced and you are seeing red. The sister is a woman you are close too and she could be two- faced, but you are not recognizing this. If someone were to slash your knees you would 'fall to your knees'.

Is this person trying to stop you from doing something in some way? I think you are now recognizing you are being brought to your knees and something very personal is being aired in public.

You shouldn't be pretending that everything is okay.

I had the most frightening dream. I was beating up a woman who I didn't recognise, although she was somehow familiar to me.

I was kicking and punching her, and I was in frenzy. The woman was crying and begging me to stop.

The scene changed and I was then sat at a table with my hand in my hair. Two nits dropped out of my hair and scuttled away. I was in a panic thinking 'I'm lousy.'

There's a situation around you involving two people and you are beating yourself up about it, not in control of your thoughts, and you don't recognise yourself. You feel you're not a good person, and you are 'lousy', and yet your inner voice is shouting at you to stop this way of thinking.

Please make an effort to get this sorted, so that the situation will be out of your hair and then you won't be infested by your thoughts.

I am a twenty years old male and in my dream I am riding a motorbike. Out of nowhere a young lady steps in front of me. She has a red hat on her head and is wearing a dark green dress. We stare intently at one and other before she turns and walks away.

I try to continue with my ride but the bike is wobbling and I am falling from side to side.

A motorbike is powerful and you need balance to ride it and at this moment you are obviously in control of yourself and well balanced. However, there is a lady around you who might stop you in your tracks. This lady is negative (dark green) and there is emotional imbalance for ahead (red on head).

Ride on in any encounter otherwise you will lose your power and control, and become unbalanced. You will recognise this person now you have been warned.

I dreamt I was in a country lane riding a peddle bike. I felt great. I looked behind and there were two people riding behind me, catching up with me. This sent me in a panic and I increased speed. I found it difficult to control the bike, the back wheel kept coming off the floor and would send me in to a slide, which was hard to correct. I felt awful but eventually saw a town up ahead. I was the first to arrive, which made me feel great again.

A peddle bike is a power. It takes hard work, a lot of effort and you need to be balanced to ride a bike but once you have mastered it you can make great progress.

You seem to be worried about people or perhaps situations 'overtaking you' and you can make mistakes in life and lose control. You see your progress as a race. Have more faith in your ability to get ahead and stay balanced.

I dreamt I was in the office and a professional looking black man was there. He held his hand out to shake hands with me. I said 'I know you but didn't realise you were working here' and he said 'I have been here three months but you didn't notice me'.

The office is you and you must be a person working with the spiritual power. The black man is a worker from spirit that has been with you for three months and although he is familiar to you, you did not recognise him. Black is a highly spiritual colour, meaning he has had many life experiences that have burnt him.

He must be a very wise and experienced worker and is with you for a particular part of your development. You are very lucky to have him with you.

I am absolutely thrilled with this interpretation as I have been trying to develop my spiritual side for some time. I feel really privileged.

In my dream a woman and her blind daughter were in front of my house, they were looking for a place to lie down. I invited them in but the woman was reluctant as she thought she would have to pay. What she didn't realise was I was not going to charge her.

They came in and my parents turned up and were annoyed that the woman and daughter were there. My father threw a box of Lego over the floor and I said 'I will have to pick that up as the blind daughter will trip over it'.

There is a situation in front of you where one person is in the dark and another person wants to lay out the truth but is frightened there will be a price to pay. This will cause conflict around you with people you are close too.

Even though there has been a deliberate attempt to trip up the person in the dark, you can put all the pieces together with a little effort.

My brother died recently, he was only thirty-three and he knew he was dying. He promised to let me know he had arrived safely on the other side but after six weeks there has been no contact.

Recently I dreamt a nurse came and took me on a journey. It involved flying and walking. I was taken to a hospital where my brother was in bed fast asleep. He looked so peaceful. I sat down and went to take his hand but the sound of activity in the street woke me. I was distraught at being woken and tried to go back in to the dream but it did not happen.

Your brother has arrived on the astral plane but his spirit is depleted and he is receiving healing. When he has gone through the healing process and had his mind unlocked, you will know he is back.

Look out for electrical interference, smell, coincidence, dreams etc., as he will contact you in subtle and cryptic ways. The nurse came to reassure you and to give you a report on his progress.

As a child I would often dream of being at the bottom of the stairs in my house and at one end of the hallway stood a bull/rhino type of animal. At the other end of the hallway was a door which I would run at and attempt to get through. Before I could the bull would charge, stopping inches short, nostrils flaring and the door would remain closed.

I am a male and am now in my early forties but I am again having that dream, though I'm still a child in it.

The house is you and as a child I would think at some stage you experienced bullying or intimidation. You probably felt there was no way out of the situation, no where to run to escape this forceful person.

Are you now experiencing this same thing again? If so, don't react but rise above the situation (climb the stairs). By doing this you will find the bull/rhino type person cannot reach you.

I have had two dreams, one after the other. The first is I am sat on a toilet in a café with people around me, although the people do not seem to be taking much notice of me. I try to hide myself as the toilet is between the serving and seating area and I am out in the open. I feel completely vulnerable and ashamed.

In the other dream I am simply on my own pushing a pram.

These two dreams are part of the same guidance. It is obvious you need to relieve yourself/pass a motion about something in your life and you are worried about the reaction of others. You need not stress about this as a café serves quick snack foods (food for thought) and no one will make a meal of your news.

This situation is obviously something that only you can push ahead with.

I came home last night and my house was securely locked with the security alarm on. Nobody else has the keys except for me. Inside the house, and on one of the stairs, was a bottle of Bach Flower Remedy called Wild Oat. Nobody had been in the house and this bottle was not in the house when I left in the morning. I have never used anything like this before. Where could it have come from and does this have a meaning?

Also, later that night my kitchen lights were turning on and off, on and off but the light switch was not moving. I feel quite freaked by these things.

You are so lucky to have received such a gift and it is called an apport – a physical gift from the spirit world sent to you in your time of need.

I have looked up Wild Oat and it is the remedy for people who feel that they want to do something worthwhile with their lives but do not know in which direction they should move. It helps people to find their true role, putting them back in touch with their own basic purpose in life so that the way ahead seems obvious.

The kitchen symbolically is where you prepare to serve; the lights were alerting you to this.

When I spoke to you on the telephone you told me you have come through an awful time and I know you have been very confused. I believe that all these life experiences will be of benefit to others and that you will be somehow working with spirit in service to mankind.

My husband died two years ago and I had a dream of him being dirty and as black as coal. I was scrubbing him to get him clean.

I have a book about dreams and it said that the dream could be warning me of imminent ill health. I also had a dream about my dead mother and she was cooking.

I haven't been feeling very well and wish I could join my husband.

When we lose a life long partner and the grief and loneliness sets in, it is very easy for us to look back at the past in an unrealistic way. We can make the person we have lost a saint, which is what you were doing by cleaning your husband. This can make us feel we can never replace that person or move on.

Your mother is representative of you and I am sure you looked after your husband very well and probably 'mothered' him. You have the ingredients to cook up something good for the future and please do not worry about your health.

I dreamt I was in a College and went down a long flight of stairs to watch a film. The film was being replayed over and over again. I got bored with this repeat performance and went outside. To my horror I fell into a lake surrounding the college. I was swept away into the water, going around and around the college, struggling to get out.

The college is you, and you have experienced a lot in your life and are learning life's lessons. However, I feel you have let yourself get down, and are stuck in the past, going over and over a situation.

A lake is symbolic of life that is stagnant, and at the moment you are going around and around. This must be quite distressing for you and this way of thinking will get you nowhere.

You need to get yourself back 'up'. If you get on with life and learn your lessons, you can be an example to others and they might benefit from your experience.

In my dream I am walking a brown dog and he is misbehaving. I let him off the lead and he runs off. I was in a real panic and was looking for him, calling to him. I was stopping people but they did not want to get involved.

A very old lady, who seemed familiar to me, told me I was wasting valuable energy on the dog and said he would return when tired and hungry. She looked at me in a very piercing way and said 'you cannot teach an old dog new tricks'.

So who is the man you are trying to control? Symbolically a dog is a man and the colour brown means of the material, someone living on earth. It must take so much energy to keep a tight rein on this person.

The old lady is someone that works with you from the world of spirit, which is why she is familiar. She is obviously very wise and the guidance she is giving you is self explanatory.

I dreamt I was in a car and I turned down a road the wrong way. I realised I had been this way before. A pick up van appeared and a guy wolf whistled. The van passed me, I gave chase and I felt exhilarated, but my eyes were closed. I started to panic and I thought, 'I am going to crash, somebody is going to get hurt. Please help me'.

The car stopped and to my amazement I was parked safely by a curb and there was a car parked next to me.

We are all vehicles, and you are in a situation you have been in before. You have responded to a man (pick up van), enjoyed the chase and have become blinded and out of control. You realised this could end in disaster, and somebody could get hurt and so in desperation you have asked for help.

You have gained control of your life with help from the person from the spirit world who is always with you. You are never alone and if you ask for help that person will work with you to help you open your eyes and learn from life.

Could you explain our son's reoccurring dream? He is standing in the middle of an empty building, almost like a warehouse or hangar. There is no-one with him and he doesn't want to run away. It's just him in the middle of a big empty space. He isn't lonely or anxious but he does have this dream often.

Also if he closes his eyes he can make himself seem "far away" and block out all surroundings. It's as if he can achieve some sort of meditation level, but it is unnerving him a little.

Both my mother and grandmother had spiritual gifts, although I do not.

Symbolically we are all buildings, houses etc., and your son is aware (warehouse) that he should be with other people. I understand that he does not feel lonely, but the guidance he is receiving through his dream is pointing out to him that he has a big empty space around him.

He seems able to block out everything around him and should be encouraged to seek the company of others.

Lately my friend is waking up and she is unable to move. She has a feeling that somebody is in the room with her. She also feels weight and heat on her paralyzed body. What does this mean?

Your friend seems to be waking up spiritually. When we are going in to or coming out of sleep we are more receptive to the spirit world, as our mind is at its' most placid. We all have someone working with us from the world of spirit, helping us to progress.

In our sleep state that person helps our spirit to sometimes leave our body and they travel with us to the astral plane where we receive guidance. Another person from the spirit world always stays with our body as a protection, and this might be who your friend is sensing in the room.

The feeling of weight and heat is experienced as your friend is waking up before the spirit is properly settled back in the body. Without the spirit being fully back in the body we are powerless to move.

I have gone through a very stressful time with my wife and strange things, such as coincidence, have been happening. I feel as though I am being guided and have an inner knowing.

This knowing seems to contradict what my wife is telling me and if I investigate, then the knowing is right and my wife has proved to be untruthful. I am quite frightened by all of this.

Why be frightened of such a wonderful gift? You are using your psychic abilities and are also being guided by someone working with you from the spirit world and you are open enough to receive the guidance.

Being open is like tuning in to a certain radio frequency and that happens when the mind is expanding, usually when you have been through adversity and gain experience.

To work with spirit enhances your life and helps you to help others.

In my dream I was in a delivery room giving birth to a baby. A midwife was there, as well as a husband and wife who were waiting to take my baby. The midwife said 'this will be easy, she has had two already'. It was an easy birth and the couple were handed my baby.

I was devastated and felt bereft, more so because the three of them completely ignored me.

I was so intrigued by your dream I had to telephone you. I discovered you were in business and it was your third attempt. Your current business is your 'baby', you have nurtured it for a long time and you are passionate about it.

You tell me you find it difficult to set boundaries with people and give a lot of your resources for free. The dream is giving you guidance, showing you that you should not give control of your baby to others. What you give for free is not appreciated and will do you harm in the long run.

In my dream I am in a run down, detached house and one of the rooms is haunted. I am going back and fore into this room where furniture and others things are moving, and a young girl appears. I keep running out frightened, but feel compelled to return and every time I go back the girl is nice to me and laughing.

The house is you and you must be haunted by something to do with a female, going over and over the situation in your mind, trying to look at it from all angles. You feel alone and perhaps 'run down'.

Don't be so hard on yourself as the girl is not stressed about things. I would say that you have to face up to the situation, let the past go with love and concentrate on healing yourself.

Thank you for this and what you have said makes perfect sense. I have recently discovered my aunty is my mother and my mother is my aunty. I have made myself ill because of this but I do know I am loved by them both, and so I will try to find some peace within.

In my dream I was at riding stables. I was allocated a horse to ride and when I got on the horses back, he spoke to me. He said 'I do not feel well, different people ride me and they pull me roughly left and right, left and right.

I felt utterly devastated for this poor horse and did not want to ride him. I tried to get help for him but was powerless as no one would listen and I was so upset.

I went to the person in charge and said I wanted to buy the horse. He gave me a price and I was arguing with him because the price seemed too high. Whilst this was taking place, someone ran to me and said 'Your horse is dying' and I was in a panic. I ran to the horse and was screaming at him not too die, as I was willing to pay the price.

Your dream is powerful and is all about power. A horse is a power (horse power) and you are being told you are giving your power away to others, letting them take over.

I would imagine this is having a devastating effect on your life.

You feel powerless to take control but the dream is explaining that you and only you should take the reins in order to gain control of your life.

I know it is not easy for you to do this and there will be a price to pay as it will be difficult, but you have no choice. If you could do this, get back in the riding seat, then things will improve.

When I was young I used to drive a fabulous, orange sports car. I had a dream the other night. I went somewhere and there was a garage. Inside the garage was my old car. I said to the person 'That's my old car' and they said 'Yes, you have left it here.' I was astounded and asked 'Do you mean it's mine?' and they said 'Of course, you just left it.'

Last night I dreamt I had my old car and I was making it roadworthy so that I could drive it.

The car is you and you are being told you are the same person you were all those years ago. You seem to have forgotten the person you were, and thought you no longer had the capabilities from when you were young.

I am glad to hear you have gotten the old you back and have taken control of your life, and are getting yourself prepared for what is ahead.

Orange is the colour of wisdom, so you can be happy you won't make any wrong choices.

My mother passed away seven months ago. I dreamt I was walking home from work and just ahead of me I saw my two cousins, my mother's sister and her husband, then behind them my mother and father.

My mother and aunty were carrying a cup of tea. They were all crossing the road, as I was walking passed them they all turned and smiled at me except my mother, who just went straight ahead. All in the dream were quite young but as I did not see my mother's face I don't know about her.

When I woke I was upset because she had not looked my way. Can you please help explain why?

You are obviously a worker, someone who helps others. Your mother is telling you to rest and refresh yourself for what is ahead.

She was always behind her family, and will be there for you when you take your new direction.

Don't look back, go straight ahead and she will guide you across the road.

I wonder if you could enlighten me on a very strange happening at my home. We are in the middle of decorating our bathroom and my husband found a drawing on the bathroom wall. I went to look and was flabbergasted at what I saw.

On the wall, about passport size, is a drawing or sketch of myself. The detail is amazing and seems to be done in charcoal. It wasn't there in the morning. Please could you shed any light on this for me?

The bathroom is symbolic of you preparing yourself for something. The message is reinforced by the decorating that is going on.

Your picture is confirming that it is you rather than your husband who is going through this transition.

This is going to be an exciting time for you and the person working with you from the world of spirit has gone to a lot of trouble to put you in the picture about what is happening.

I am going through a dreadful time at the moment, my wife has left me for a friend of our family and I cannot seem to move forward. I have completely lost my faith in everything and everyone.

This has coincided with a reoccurring dream where I see myself in bed and realise that my pillow is wedged between the side of the bed and a small cabinet.

I am so sorry to hear of your loss and can quite understand why you feel vulnerable and alone with no support or connection to the higher power.

A pillow is a support for ahead and that support is now by your side. Be confident that those who work with you from the spirit world will never let you down and when you need them most, they are there for you.

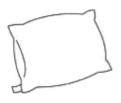

I am having an awful time and really weird things are happening.

I met a man I felt was my soul mate, sent to me by my family in spirit. He came in to my life at just the right time, when I needed help, and through him my life has been sorted.

I recently found out he was seeing another woman and the effect on me was terrible. I went mad and screamed at the walls and was shouting at my family in spirit 'why did you let me believe he was my soul mate'.

I went to bed and heard an almighty crash from the hallway. When I investigated, an artificial plant that hangs on the wall and is as light as a feather, was spread across the floor.

Your family in spirit have symbolically spoken to you. They have told you 'it was a plant, it was not the real thing'. They sent you help when you needed it.

How fantastic.

In my dream I was at a pond. The pond had a fountain in the middle and there were flowers and it looked very pretty. Fish were in the pond and they were all vivid colours and really large.

I was stood at the pond with a fishing rod trying to catch these fish, and I knew that once caught, I needed to put them somewhere else. These fish were too beautiful to swim in such a small amount of water.

However, they would not bite my bait and I felt so frustrated.

Water represents life and we should all be in the sea of life, as a pond is so very restrictive, and does not give us a lot of potential for growth.

I would imagine there are people who you care about who are in stagnant situations. You feel that they need help and you are trying to get them to move on.

However, they seem quite happy with their situation and you have to learn that they must help themselves.

In my dream I seem to be working very hard to get somewhere until I remember that I am a powerful white witch and all I have to do is think myself where I want to be. Sometimes I end up saving everyone by saying a powerful spell that stops all the malevolent people going around in disguise stealing children etc.

Why am I having these dreams? I would appreciate an explanation.

Your dream is about self development, you are working hard to get to where you want to be.

I would imagine that you are a very good person and have the best of intentions for others. You are being reminded that the power of the mind is awesome and you can achieve what you want by willpower and determination

I am sure that you have a strong sense of what is right and wrong and you want to make a difference to this world. I hope this makes sense to you and I am sure you will succeed in your mission.

I thought I awoke three times from a dream, but must have been dreaming.

The first time I got out of bed and noticed all the furniture had changed. The second time was the same; I looked downstairs and saw a rocking horse in the hall. The third time, all my own possessions were gone and different furniture was there, I again looked down the stairs and this time there was a pram in the hall.

Still going on with my dream, I returned back to bed and finally woke up and everything was back to normal.

I am eight-six years of age and often wondered what was the meaning of this strange dream I had many years ago?

At the time of your dream you must have been going through a reluctant change, going back and fore in your mind, thinking of changes that needed to be made.

When you had finally made up your mind you were being shown that you could push ahead with the new situation.

In my dream I was told that there was a fire in the hallway of my sisters house. I ran to the house and my sister was there with a friend. I realised what was burning was paperwork to do with a business that I planned to start, and there were people examining and picking through these papers.

My sister said she was sorry but she and her friend were smoking and that caused the fire. She left me to pick up all my charred papers.

The hallway (passage) is to do with time and I believe this is something ahead of you, as your business has not yet started.

Who is the person that is like a sister to you? She is sharing your emotional business with others, picking over the details, and this could have an effect on your well being as a cigarette is a health warning.

Please be careful who you confide in and do not give them the opportunity to cause problems for you. Forewarned is forearmed.

I dreamt I was in a house and I fell. I hit the floor and smacked my face. My head kept bouncing back, and I smacked my face repeatedly.

Eventually I got up but realised there were people around. I was so embarrassed, and pretended I was alright, even though I had been hurt.

I went to the kitchen and opened the fridge, took out a jug of milk and dropped it. The milk went everywhere and I was so upset, my body seemed to shrink.

The house is you, and there is something that's smacking you in the face, it's a situation that's hurt you, but you are pretending everything is okay.

My advice would be that you acknowledge this situation. The kitchen is symbolic of our preparation to serve others, and it's no good crying over spilt milk, what is done is done.

Once you deal with the incident, learn from it and then let it go. In that way you will grow as a person and your experience might benefit others.

I am off work with stress, as there are four people in my workplace up to no good and I have found out about this. I am being bullied and victimised by them.

Last week I was sleeping on my stomach in bed. I woke up and on the head board in front of me were four spiders. It was as though they felt me looking at them and they ran away.

I am terrified of spiders and so I moved to another room and exactly the same thing happened.

What's in your bed is in your life and the head board represents something ahead.

Spiders are symbolic of deceitful people 'Oh what a tangled web we weave whilst trying to deceive'.

The four people you mentioned are weaving a web to trap you but, forewarned is forearmed.

Speak to the people in authority about what you know otherwise you may find that your colleagues have plotted to discredit you.

What fantastic guidance you have been given.

On two separate occasions I have woken up from sleep and realised that I could not move. I was unable to open my eyes or mouth, and could not move my limbs. It was truly frightening and felt as though there was a pressure bearing down on my body.

I am now frightened to go to sleep as I have been told by a friend that this is a 'pin down' by a spirit entity.

Let me assure you you're not being pinned down by a spirit entity.

When asleep our spirit sometimes leaves the body and goes to the astral plane, where we receive guidance for our earthly problems.

You have woken up too soon, when the spirit is in the half way stage, neither in nor out of the body. Without the spirit the body has no animation and is rather like a vehicle that cannot move until the driver is in place.

I understand that you are frightened but I can assure you there is no need to be.

In my dream my car was stolen. I was absolutely distraught as I use my car for work and so many people rely on me.

I went to the police station for help and the police were ignoring me. I left the station and saw a black lady driving my car. She looked at me and waved to me.

We are all cars and the fact your car is used for work shows you are a worker, the type of person who is always helping and carrying others.

Your dream suggests you've been hurt emotionally. The colour black symbolizes a person who has been burnt and is very wise because of it. This hurt has changed you, and a part of who you are or were, has gone for ever.

The higher power won't help you with this as it is obviously something you need to go through to change and take control of you.

I believe you are already recognizing this change as the black lady, the new you, waved at you.

I have been having disquiet about my relationship and have been asking questions of the universe, 'should I be with this man'?

The other day I lay on the bed to meditate. I fell asleep and felt myself being awoken with a nudge to my side. I then felt hands around my throat and it was as though I was being strangled. I tried to fight it off but could not get these hands from my throat.

This felt so real it was like I was semi conscious and I am now frightened as I am thinking I have attracted bad spirits to me.

The power of the universe is awesome. You asked a question about your relationship and you were answered.

You were given a nudge by those that are working with you from spirit, and they were showing you that you are being strangled.

Do not be frightened, I can assure you that you have not attracted any negative energy but you asked a question and you have simply been answered.

In my dream I was a teacher and I was going to this farm to teach the animals. As I was walking to the farm with the farmer there was a path and he said 'you should not go down that path'. I found it difficult not to give way to temptation and take that path but he shepherded me away.

The building that I was to work from was a converted barn, and as I approached all the animals were flocking around me.

I presume that in your life you have nearly taken the wrong path but the person that works with you from spirit has been able to guide you, to keep you from that path.

You have been converted. The animals are people and there must be those around you who can benefit from your experience and are eager to learn. You can teach them the right way.

Having just phoned you to ask your story you tell me you are now working in a drug unit. Well done.

I was dreaming I lived in a terraced house. I was looking out the back garden, and it was an awful mess. There were lots of shallow holes, with mud banked at the sides, as though someone had started digging and then left to dig somewhere else.

I looked to my left and in a neighbouring garden my mother was stood waving; she was hanging washing on the line.

To my right my aunty was in another garden, climbing into a hot air balloon. I walked to the front of the house, looked out the window and there was a 'For Sale' sign being erected.

The house is you, attached to a group of people who are family, or like family. The back is the past and you have lots of unresolved issues, which have left things in a bit of a mess.

There is dirty washing being aired in public and things are up in the air. You are being told it is time for you to move on.

I am getting married in October and I dreamt I was not prepared.

The day arrived and my hair was greasy yellow and I had not booked a hair appointment. I put my dress on but hadn't bought a new bra and had to wear this grubby bra. It started raining and the horses arrived. The carriage wasn't decorated so I had to help with that in my dress and I eventually arrived in church like a drowned rat.

A wedding represents a new way of life. Perhaps the wedding has taken priority and you have not prepared for after the event?

Hair also represents something for ahead and you had forgotten to make the time to organize and plan for ahead, and get everything in order. A bra is something to uplift you for ahead, again this is neglected. A horse is a power 'horse power' and it is there to work with you, to take you to a destination and, again, what the horse is prepared to pull is not ready.

Perhaps you should take a good look at what your plans will be for after the event.

My mother died six months ago and I am devastated. She was always there for me and gave me such fabulous guidance. I am not a very wise person and my life has been littered with disasters of my own making.

Initially I used to resent my mothers interference but over the last year of her life I have been grateful for her input. She came to me last night in a dream. I asked her "Where have you been?" and she said "Only in the room next door". She had an apple in her hand and she offered it to me.

Your mother is letting you know she has survived and is still close to you; she's just in the next room. Although you cannot see her, she can continue to communicate with you.

An apple represents a teacher and your mother is offering you her wisdom. She can still teach and guide you. Accept what she is offering and listen to your inner voice. If you listen she will never let you down.

I have had the most peculiar dream. In my dream I was in a bathroom and there was an aquarium full of fish. They were all looking at me.

I felt I was in a rush as I needed to go to the bank but a very large baby appeared and I had to take it with me. I picked up the baby but it was so heavy. I knew I wouldn't get to the bank as the baby was too heavy for me to carry and I was reluctant to put it down.

Fish represent people and an aquarium is people who are confined. You are in a situation where you are confined and you recognise this. You have the opportunity to prepare yourself or get ready for something.

You need to put down whatever it is you are carrying as it will hold you back and confine you.

A bank is a source of power and so if you put down the baby you will be empowered for what's ahead.

My beloved sister died In November of last year. She was only forty-nine. At her funeral a butterfly was hovering around my shoulder. It was with me as I walked into the church and re-appeared when I left the church.

It was a dismal, dark day but as we left the church the sun came out and lit up everything.

I cannot get these events out of my mind and recognise that a butterfly should not be around in November. I wondered if there was a spiritual explanation.

I am so sorry to hear of your loss but you are right, there is a spiritual explanation to these events.

A butterfly is a fantastic symbol. It starts life as a caterpillar and then forms into a chrysalis and emerges as a butterfly. It is a symbol of transformation and the struggle from one life to another.

Your sister has made that transformation and she is free. She is enjoying the warmth and brightness of her new surroundings and she wanted you to know that.

I dreamt I was in my house and there was a knocking at the front door. I was sat comfortable and didn't want to answer the door. I felt guilty as the knocking was persistent but still I sat.

The dream changed and I was in a prison. I could walk around quite freely from one cell to the next and I was really happy in the prison.

There was a nice bed in one of the cells and I lay down on the bed and went to sleep. I could see myself in this bed, snoring away.

There is an opportunity knocking, or an opening in life for you, but you are content to be confined in a prison of your own making. You feel guilty about your lack of motivation but still you confine yourself.

I am sure this is something you are aware of as you can see yourself quite happily sleeping, but you will never reach your true potential by staying in this prison. Open the door and let opportunity in.

In my dream I was in my kitchen working away, chopping up lots of fruit and vegetables. I was really happy as I was preparing for something.

On the counter was a rat in a cage. It was enormous and I was talking to it. It seemed I had just caught the rat and I was very satisfied. I looked out the window into the back garden and there was a bull glaring at me but I waved it away. When I looked back at the rat there was a large spider in the cage as well.

I am normally frightened of rats, spiders and bulls and cannot understand why I would dream of them.

The kitchen is symbolic of preparing to serve others, and you are putting a lot of effort into your preparation.

I believe you have been bullied in the past but have overcome that experience. A rat and spider represent untrustworthy people but you have managed to contain them and I am confident all this has prepared you for what's ahead.

I dreamt I was sat at a table with my family and I had a steaming bowl of food in front of me.

I was the only one with food and I was being encouraged by the others to eat. I tried to swallow some food but it was too hot and I started to choke.

Someone gave me a drink but I continued to choke. I was then given a biscuit to dip in my drink but I just could not swallow it and continued choking.

My teeth started falling out and blood was running from my mouth.

There is a situation around you where you are being served something that is too hot for you to swallow. Those involved have tried to dilute the impact on you but still you cannot swallow it. Even when they try to soften the news, you cannot swallow it.

Teeth are words and you are reacting with emotion, saying things that you probably wouldn't normally say. You need to sit and think calmly about the situation.

I had a dream where I was in my house, although it is not like the house I live in, but I knew it was my house. There were patio doors in my bedroom leading on to a wide balcony. There was an amazing view of the sea.

I was sat on the balcony watching my daughter doing ballet. She was up on her toes and gracefully dancing around. Then my father, who has been dead for years, came in. He smiled at me and was smoking a cigar.

The house is you and you don't recognise how changed you now are. You have a wonderful view on life.

Your daughter represents the intuitive and spiritual side of you which is growing. There is a need to keep on your toes as your father brought you a warning about the material, as a cigar represents the material.

Use your intuition in any situations around you and ask your father for help. I am confident your growing wisdom will not let you down.

In my dream I was judging two lines of ladies and I picked out a lady with beautiful brown eyes as the winner.

I was looking across the Bristol Channel when a ship left the port across the sea and headed straight for me. It was going too fast and it eventually beached in front of me. I pushed the ship off the beach. The ship stopped and a junior male crew member came off the ship, game me a present and returned to the ship. Then a senior male crew member came off the ship, gave me a gift before returning to the ship. The ship then appeared to head straight back to its original post.

For your information, I have family living across the channel who have had problems in the past four years, and I have tried to help them.

You have had to judge a situation and you decided that the person who viewed things in a more material way was right. You have obviously helped your family get back into the sea of life.

Symbolically your efforts are being acknowledged. Well done.

I am having night terrors. I go to sleep but start to wake up and I am paralysed. I can't move my body or open my eyes. A horrible, demon like man is with me and he stands before me and I am frightened of him. I have tried to ignore him but that makes him mad and he jumps up and down, shaking his fists at me. His appearance is absolutely grotesque.

I am frightened of going to sleep at night.

I am so sorry to hear of this distressing experience and can understand why you are frightened.

Your spirit is coming out of the body and you are partially waking when the spirit isn't completely free. This is so the experience will have a deeper impact on you. You are being told you need to confront your demons. Only you can know what your demon is but it will be a weakness, something you have allowed to control you.

The next time this happens speak to the demon with your mind and tell him you want to confront him and ask for his help.

In my dream my ex-husbands first wife came to me and she was heavily pregnant. I took her to the edge of the sea and was waiting for a speed boat to come so I could teach this pregnant lady to ski.

We stood looking at the sea and an enormous wave was coming towards us. The lady went to run but I told her 'no' we must stay where we are. Miraculously the wave went over our heads and crashed behind us. The lady was tired and lay down on the floor and from nowhere I produced two pillows to make her comfortable.

The ex-wife is a weaker aspect of your personality that you have been carrying around.

Sea is life and the strong part of you is showing the weaker part how to stand up in life, symbolised by the skis. You have learnt you cannot be afraid of life and are resisting the impulse to run when the going gets tough.

You are now supporting this part of you in preparation for a new beginning, as a pillow is a support for ahead.

I was dreaming I was on an aeroplane, waiting for it to take off. Sat next to me was the partner of my solicitor. We were stressing because my solicitor was not on board.

The plane started to taxi down the run way and was picking up speed, going faster and faster when I noticed the door was open. I shouted for help and the pilot brought the plane to a halt.

The dream then changed and I was on my own pushing a pram, although I was quite obviously heavily pregnant.

There must be a situation around you where you need your solicitor or some kind of legal representation 'on board', or perhaps you need to take the legal issues 'on board', otherwise you will leave yourself open and what ever you are working on will not take off.

Only then will you be able to 'push ahead' with what ever it is you have been carrying around with you. Good luck with your venture and it seems to be something that is almost ready to be born.

I dreamt I was in my house and one of the living room walls had moved. My living room was really big and I ran to the next room and saw this was now small. I couldn't believe that this had happened nor could I understand how.

I pushed the wall and was shocked to discover it was on castors. I could now push the wall back to where it should have been.

However, I could not remember where that was and so I had to use my senses and was trying to think if it felt right in certain positions.

Your dream is about boundaries. I would imagine the theme throughout your life has been about setting and keeping boundaries with people in place. You are doing it again, and it has happened without you knowing, but it is not wise.

Listen to your inner voice or sixth sense and let that guide you in setting boundaries.

You're absolutely right I do have a problem with boundaries with people, and I really am going to try and do better. Thank you for the guidance.

I am writing to you to see if you can explain a dream I have had for many years.

I am always late and getting lost. I struggle to be in a certain place for a certain time and lots of things seem to stop me getting there i.e. buses not going the right way etc. It progressed throughout working (not being able to get to work). It stopped for a short time after taking a course that interested me greatly, but still occurs occasionally.

I have looked in many dream books and never found 'late' or 'lost' in them. Hoping you can help.

I believe that you have the potential to do a lot with your life. Are you particularly talented or clever in some area? If so, you are not motivated to do the hard work necessary, or are easily distracted.

It is interesting to note when you did do a course that the dream stopped. You should 'get out there' and achieve your true potential. It's still not too late.

In my dream I was walking barefoot on shale and my feet were cut. There were people walking with stout shoes on and there was track beneath their feet. I was crying 'how on earth did this happen to me?' and trying to get off the shale.

I realised I had a bike with me, but I wasn't riding it. It took some effort to get on the bike, and peddling with my cut feet over this uneven ground was very difficult. However, I started to make some headway.

I was concentrating on peddling when the dream ended.

Feet, shoes and what is underfoot are all to do with our direction.

You have no protection for your direction as you haven't been using the power at your disposal.

I am glad to hear you have realised you have resources on hand that, although hard work, can get you to be where you are supposed to be, back on track.

I have had an horrendous three years. My wife is constantly leaving me and I feel so insecure and vulnerable. She refuses to discuss things with me and I am desperate to save my marriage.

Weird things have been happening lately. I keep hearing the sound of a cuckoo. No one else hears it, only me. I have now started dreaming of a nest with three birds in that all look the same, and then suddenly one of the birds stretches its neck and makes the noise of a cuckoo. Can you please explain this for me?

A cuckoo is a person and it could be you are being cuckolded. Are there three people in your relationship? There are connotations of helplessness and humiliation attributed to the word cuckoo or cuckold, and from what you say I would imagine you have these feelings.

Perhaps you should take control of what is happening and make an effort to find out what is going on. You need to empower yourself by gaining knowledge.

I have recently lost my mother. She was only sixty-two and her death was unexpected. I am broken hearted. I have been having a reoccurring dream about her.

I am downstairs in my house and I hear her calling me from upstairs. I run up the stairs and into my bedroom. My mother is stood, with her arms held out to me. I run to her and we cuddle and kiss one and other. She tells me she will never leave me but then I wake up and she's not there.

Symbolically we are all houses, we house our spirit. Your bedroom represents what is around you in life and your mother is letting you know she is around you and she can communicate with you mind to mind. Climbing the stairs is symbolic of the mind and thinking on a higher level.

Make time to sit in the quiet and speak to her in your mind. Ask her for help, strength and guidance and she will be happy to influence you.

In my dream I was with a lady and we had a baby. It belonged to both of us and we were taking it in turns to push the baby in its pram.

When it was her turn she would put a cover or some kind of wrap on its head. When it was my turn I would take the cover off, but I would do this in a placating way, like as though she was in charge.

This was the theme of the dream, with her in a position of dominance and me trying to assert myself, but not quite succeeding.

You are in a partnership or some kind of joint venture with someone. You are both trying to push ahead with your baby, or your project, but whereas you want things to be out in the open for ahead, your partner wants to cover something up.

Perhaps your partner feels things would be too exposed if the wraps were off. As it is both your baby you should insist on an equal say.

I had a dream where I was sitting naked on the settee in my front room. I was horrified as my daughter was also in the room. However, my daughter seemed completely indifferent to my nakedness and was chatting away happily.

The television was on and I saw the gates of a cemetery. "I recognise those gates" I thought, and was immediately transported to them. I found myself standing with my husband and children, looking through the gates at the cemetery beyond. I said to my husband "I want to go inside and find our graves" but he refused. I left him and the children and entered the Cemetery.

I made my way to a building and inside was an old man pawing over a thick ledger. I gave him my husband's name and asked him where the grave was. The old man was running his fingers up and down columns, turning over the pages, obviously having difficulty in finding the grave.

After a while he pushed a ledger towards me and I opened it. There on a card that was taped to the inside page of the book was my name saying 'she was a good person'.

Firstly, it is obvious that you would be horrified to 'bare all' to your daughter (bare your soul). Is there something you do not want your daughter to know? If so, don't worry as your girl will take it in her stride and be at ease with it.

Television is communication and a cemetery is where you put things to rest. Perhaps you want out of your marriage and your husband doesn't? The book that the old man was pawing over is the book of the dead and he could not find your husband's name mentioned. Passing the book to you shows that you need to see for yourself that to continue with the marriage could be the death of you (the death of the person that you are), and your husband is not affected by the stresses in the marriage.

As your name was taped in the book, you are not meant to suffer this way as you are a good person.

In my dream my next door neighbour was in my house and was offering me a glass of water but it had some kind of drug in it.

I refused the glass saying I didn't want to take the drugs as I knew it was not good for me, but he was insisting and was making an issue of it.

It took all my willpower to say no, and eventually after a lot of pushing and shoving I was able to get him out of the house. I closed the door but he somehow opened it again but I forced the door shut. Once shut I locked and bolted it.

The house is you and the next door neighbour is someone close to you that you have been addicted too. I think this person has been like a drug to you but thank goodness you are recognising this.

Keep the door to 'you' shut and bolted, otherwise he might force his way back in and you could become addicted again.

Good luck and stay strong.

I was dreaming I was handed an envelope and when I opened the envelope there were photos of my husband enjoying himself at a funfair.

My husband has been having an affair in real life and in my dream I was bemused as his girlfriends was not with him.

I was fretting that he was at the funfair and then he appeared out of nowhere. He took the photos off me and tried to hide them. He said they were forgeries.

Your husband has been enjoying the thrill of the ride, he's had a load of fun but it doesn't seem his girlfriend is a consideration. He's not worried about her but it is his enjoyment that is important.

This is a side of him that is not very attractive and he will do his best to hide it from you.

Please stop fretting and do some serious thinking as you deserve better than this.

My mother died a year ago and I have felt so alone, even though I have two beautiful young children. Five months ago I met a lovely man, and he moved in with me three months ago. Since he moved in weird things have started to happen in my home.

The burglar alarm goes off for no reason, and the door bell rings and there is no one there. These things I could live with and, in fact, might have thought it was my mum letting me know she was around but after each happening there is a dreadful smell.

I have heard this might be poltergeist activity and we are now quite frightened. Do you think we should move house?

Your first thought about your mother being responsible for these events is probably right.

An alarm is a warning you should take heed of. Something doesn't smell good in your home and your mother is telling you to open up to her. Even though she is no longer with you in the physical body, she can still be of help to you from her world.

She still loves you and your children and has your best interests at heart.

I was woken from sleep and there was a parrot on my bed. It was talking away and I couldn't hear what it was saying but I felt comfortable with it, as it was friendly. I then fell back to sleep.

You are being told 'wake up'. What is in your bed is in your life. Who is the friend you are telling all your business too? A parrot is a person who repeats, and this friend is repeating all you tell them.

In my dream I was stood with a person and we were really close. In fact we were so close our skin was rubbing against each other. I then realised my skin was blistered.

Someone you are close too is rubbing you up the wrong way, really irritating you and getting under your skin. The guidance you are being given is 'move away from them'.

I have had a terrifying dream where I am being raped. I make no attempt to defend myself and allow it to happen.

Someone is violating you and forcing you in to a situation where you are vulnerable. You are allowing this to happen and you should take control and defend yourself.

I am always being chased in my dreams and who ever is running after me never catches me but I am left feeling thoroughly tired.

You are running away from a person or a situation. Perhaps it is about time you stood your ground and confronted this issue, as to continue in this way will take all your energy.

I keep dreaming of the toilet and I always have a real need to urinate but when I enter the cubicle the toilet is filthy and I can't go.

There is something you need to relieve yourself of but you can't bring yourself to do it. It is not comfortable for you to be in this situation and although your need is desperate, you have a horror of letting this situation go. Please talk about it so that you can find relief.

I have been dreaming of a woman who stands at the side of my bed and she seems familiar to me. She is really ugly with a gaping mouth and she seems to be talking incessantly.

The woman is a part of you that you need to face. I feel you are nagging and the words are ugly. Take a good look at yourself.

74

TWO

A – Z

OF

SYMBOLS

AND THEIR MEANING

Abscess   Poisonous feelings within –
open up and let it out.

Ace   A surprise up your sleeve by
holding the ace card/an expert in a given
field.

Acrobat   A flexible person or situation.

Actor   A person masking their
feelings/playing a part.

Aerial   A transmitter and receiver of
information.

Agent   Someone who works for others.

*Double agent – a person who will double
cross you.*

Aircraft   We are all aircraft, we can take
off and be up in the air at the slightest thing.

*Aeroplane - a person taking off in a
measured way, as they have control over
their emotions.*

Flight - being uplifted. Take flight.

Helicopter - someone taking off, and lifting themselves up/rise above

things. Caution, you might *take off too quickly and find yourself 'up in the air'.*

Parachute - a person or a situation to prevent you from falling and ensure a safe landing.

Alarm   A   warning/something   to   be alarmed about.

Alien   A   strange   person/a   strange situation.

Alleyway   A way out but you need to be careful/a short cut.

Angel   A messenger bringing spiritual help and guidance.

Earth angel – a kind and giving person.

Animals   We are all animals – life is a jungle out there.

Ape – copying someone/a person messing around.

Ass - a fool.

Bear – a person of great strength who is a comfort.

Buffalo - a strong person/a good provider.

Bull – a bully/a person born in the sign of Taurus/tactless person.

Camel - a person who has the hump.

Cat – a woman.

Cheetah – a woman who cheats.

Cow - mother or mother figure.

Dalmatian dog – a man who is spot on.

Dog – a man.

Dog bark - a male whose bark is worse than his bite.

Donkey - a person that is put upon/a worker.

Elephant – a loyal, family orientated female.

Foal - someone just coming in to their spiritual power.

Fox – a cunning person.

Gazelle – an alert person.

Giraffe – someone who stretches themselves when reaching for spiritual food and knowledge.

Goat – grandfather/a person born in the sign of Capricorn.

Guide dog – a man who gives others the confidence to move forward in life by helping them to see things clearly.

Hamster - someone that takes spiritual food and stores it, they digest it at their own pace.

Hen – a motherly person.

Herd - a group of people of like minds.

Hog – A greedy male/someone hogging the limelight.

Horse – power/horse power.

Kangaroo – a person carrying a responsibility that is coming along in leaps and bounds/an Australian.

Kitten – a young female.

Leopard – a person who cannot change its spots or ways.

Lion – a person born in the sign of Leo/a leader/a strong person.

Lioness - a protector, she looks after the family.

Mole – a person working underground – a spy.

Monkey - a person who is up to no good/monkeying around.

Mouse – a timid female not to be trusted.

Mouse trap – a female trapped by her own actions.

Mule – a person put upon by others/a stubborn person.

Mutton - mutton dressed up as lamb/a tough person.

Pack - an organised group of people who hunt and run together/pack away something that has been on your mind.

Penguin – a person who is emotionally cold and sees everything in black and white/a formal male.

Pig – a person who is happy and content with their lot/a pig of a person.

Poodle – a pampered man.

Porcupine – a prickly person who has to be handled with care.

Puppy – a young male.

Python – a person who will squeeze the life out of you.

Rabbit - someone rabbiting on.

Ram – a person born in the sign of Aries/a person who will batter down your resolve/a nasty man.

Rat - a despicable man/someone who keeps gnawing away at you.

Rhinoceros – someone who is thick skinned.

Sheep - a follower of others/someone who is easily led.

Sheep dog – a man who guides and brings others together.

Snake – an untrustworthy person/symbol of healing.

Squirrel – a person who hoards things.

Tiger – a passionate person/a person quick to pounce.

Tortoise – a person with a hard shell/a person who takes their time but gets there in the end.

Weasel – a person who always weasels out of a situation.

Wolf – a man not to be trusted.

Antique   Someone of great value from the past.

Apostle   A spiritual person in service to others.

Archer   A person who will target you. A person born in the sign of Sagittarius.

Arrow   Pointing the way.

Asleep   Missing out on life.

Assault   A person or situation that is getting at you.

Asylum   Seeking a place of safety.

Athlete   Fit   person/someone   getting ahead/in training

Atlas   Finding a direction in life – showing you where you are/the world is in your hands.

Attic   The mind.

Axis   Keeps something balanced.

Baby   A new beginning or happening/something you're passionate about and you carry with you.

Baby's napkin – a new situation that needs to be covered up as it is private.

Baby's rattle – a new situation that will rattle you.

Back   The past/something behind us.

Badge   Identifying someone.

Bag   Something personal that you keep close/carrying baggage.

Balcony   A person who extends their view on life.

Ball   A person who can bounce back/someone who is up and down.

Beach ball – a colourful and bouncy person.

Football – someone who has been kicked about/kicked into touch.

Golf ball – A situation in which you may end up in a hole.

Rugby ball – Something you have in hand that you need to pass on.

Tennis ball – a situation between two people.

Ballerina   A person who is always on their toes/well balanced.

Balloon   A need or ability to rise above a situation.

Hot air balloon - talking a lot of hot air/up in the air about something.

Band   A group of people who are in harmony/banding together.

Banner   A declaration for all to see.

Bar   Serves spirit.

Barmaid - someone serving spirit.

Barrel - a person who is a barrel of laughs.

Bare   Something or someone who is exposed.

Base   A strong foundation.

Basket   A lot of weaving has gone in to a basket - linked with the family (wood).

Basket of fruit - fruits of your labour.

Bath   Preparing you for something.

Bathroom   Place of preparation.

Battery   A person that gives others strength/a person that needs recharging.

Battle   A problem or a situation.

Battlefield - a problem or situation that could hurt many people.

Beach   Beach is to do with life.

Pebbly beach – watch where you're going.

Sand - time.

Beard   A person who is hiding behind something/wont face up to things.

Beaten up   Beating yourself up/being hard on yourself or others.

Bed   What's in your bed is in your life. If somebody gets in your bed they are in your life. How do they make you feel?

Bed bug – an annoying person, they will drain you.

Four poster bed – support in life.

Headboard – something for ahead.

Mattress – your foundation in life.

Pillow - support for ahead.

Untidy bed – untidy life.

Bedcover   What's covering you in life. You have to look at the type of cover.

Blanket - hiding the truth/a comfort.

Blanket box - a person with lots of comfort to give to others.

Candlewick bedspread – life is not smooth.

Tapestry bedspread – a colourful life.

87

Bedroom   Things going on around you in life.

Beggar   Someone who takes from others.

Binoculars   Take a closer look at a person or situation.

Birds   We are all birds.

Albatross - a warning about life.

Aviary - people confined in a small place.

Beak - someone who is beaky/keep your beak out.

Bird – a woman.

Bird cage - trapped in a situation/someone feeling caged.

Birds nest – a person who has put a lot of work into the home to make it comfortable and safe for their young/a person feathering their nest.

Black bird – a spiritual and caring person.

Blue tit - a woman whose blue.

Budgie – a person that is chirpy in life.

Buzzard – a person who will pick your bones or the bones of a situation.

Chicken - a cowardly person/a child.

Crow – someone who is constantly crowing about something.

Cuckoo - a crazy person/a person who has been cuckolded/exploitation.

Dove – a person bringing or offering peace.

Duck – a person on top of life.

Eagle – a person able to rise above a situation and see things more clearly.

Emu – a steady person who is not a high flyer.

Falcon – a person who attacks those weaker than themselves.

Fledgling - someone who is learning – just starting out in life.

Goose – a silly person who does not think.

Gosling – someone who is growing and learning how to stay on top of life.

Hawk – a person who doesn't miss a thing.

Hen – 'mother hen', someone who looks after her brood/trys to get the whole world under her wings.

King fisher - someone who is of great importance.

Lark – a person who larks about.

Magpie - a person who is attracted to things that are shiny and new/someone who talks incessantly.

Nest egg - someone with power in reserve.

Nightingale - a person who speaks beautiful words when you are in the dark.

Ostrich – someone burying their head in the sand.

Owl - a wise person

Parrot - a person that repeats/be careful who you confide in.

Peacock – proud person who shows their true colours and likes to be heard.

Pheasant – someone game for anything.

Pigeon – a messenger.

Robin red breast – a person who keeps the flame alight (spiritual flame) and makes sacrifices for others.

Rook – be careful this person will rook you.

Seagull – a person who is gullible.

Sparrow – a chirpy person who is a survivor in life, never letting things get them down.

Stork – a well balanced person with great expectations.

Swallow – someone who needs to swallow their words or pride.

Swan – a person who is swanning along in life/a stately person.

Vulture – a person who is a scavenger/a person picking over the pieces.

Woodpecker – a family member who will wear you down by constantly pecking at you.

Blackboard   Something to be taught/an aid to help you learn or teach.

Black person   Person with lots of life experience as they have been burnt/ someone who is highly spiritual/a healer.

Blind person   Someone who is in the dark/cannot see.

Blister   A person or situation that has rubbed you up the wrong way/friction.

Blood   Seeing red/anger/not in control.

Boats   We are all vessels on the sea of life.

Anchor - something to anchor you/pull up anchor and move on.

Ark - a person offering safety or support for those seeking refuge.

Canoe – *paddle your own canoe and get on with life/a balanced person.*

Cruiser – *a popular person able to cruise through life.*

Dinghy – *a person whose ego is easily inflated.*

Ferry – *a person always helping others.*

Fleet – *a lot of people working together in life.*

Galleon - *a person going to war. Able to defend.*

Gondola – *a romantic person.*

Lifeboat – *a helper/person who rescues people when they are in need.*

Liner – *someone who carries a lot of people.*

Navigator - *a person who steers others through life.*

Oar – *something on hand to help you steer through the sea of life.*

Pirate - *a person who takes from others.*

93

Raft – a person who throws you a life raft when life is stormy.

Sailor – someone who sails through life.

Steamboat – go at a steady pace under your own steam.

Submarine – a person who is easily depressed, going down to the depths of despair, but always able to rise back up again.

Tugboat – always pulling people along.

Wreck – a person who has been through the storms of life and is a nervous wreck.

Yacht – a person working with the power/make sure you are in control at the helm/a balanced person.

Bollard   To stop you from straying/keep you from crossing the barrier.

Bomb   Explosive situation.

Book   We are all books.

Bible – a religious person.

Book case - different chapters in your life/a group of people/someone who holds a lot of wisdom.

Chapter – a period of your life.

Closed book - closed person.

Dictionary - a person of letters/a person with a large vocabulary.

Directory - a person with many contacts.

Encyclopaedia - a very knowledgeable person.

Guide book – a person giving guidance to others.

Novel - a novel or different person or situation/a person whose story is made up, but is entertaining all the same.

Open book - open person.

Page – a part of your life.

Scrapbook – a person who holds onto things from the past that should be scrapped.

Story book – a person who has a story to tell.

Well worn book – a person who has seen a lot of life and is worn down.

Yellow book – a positive person.

Bottle   A person/bottling things up.

Green bottle– a negative person.

Box   A person or situation that is boxed in/confined.

Boxer   A person who is a fighter in life.

Bracelet   Something   around   you/ something already there on hand.

Brake   Put the brakes on/slow down.

Brass   Top brass/the best.

Brew   Something brewing.

Brick   A solid and dependable person.

Bridge   Bridging a gap/a link.

Briefcase   A person who comes straight to the point and is brief/legal representation.

Broom   A person sweeping away the rubbish in life/a new broom sweeps clean.

Bucket   A helper/carrying others or the means to help in a situation.

Buildings   We are all buildings.

Betting office - someone who takes lots of gambles in life.

Building for sale – a person who needs to move on.

Bungalow – someone who is on the level, what you see is what you get.

Castle – a strong person with solid boundaries, they can open them self to others when they want.

Church - A spiritual person – any form of religious building represents this.

Cinema – a person entertaining others.

Coal shed - old power. Full shed spiritually stocked/empty shed you have given so much and left nothing for yourself.

College - a person with a lot of knowledge, who is willing to teach others.

Converted building – a person who has been converted.

Cottage - a person who is popular/brings peace and comfort.

Council housing estate – a person who is in a state and needs counselling.

Detached house – a person who stands alone.

Eiffel tower - a tall person, could be French.

Factory - a person with a lot of output.

Flat – a person who feels flat.

Fort - a person with a lot of protection/ someone who is difficult to get in to.

Hospital – a person of great compassion who heals all types of people.

Hostel – a person taking others in when they are at their most vulnerable.

Hotel – an hospitable person giving short term help to many.

House – We are all houses, we house our spirit.

Housing estate – a person in a state about something.

Hovel – A person who does not take care of themselves.

Lighthouse - a person who has a bright light and is always there to help people (ships) in a storm, to prevent them going on the rocks.

Mansion – a dignified person.

Mill - someone who is going through the mill.

Offices - a group of people linked with work – spiritual work.

Palace – a regal and well respected person.

Penthouse – a person with pent up emotions.

Prison - a state of mind – imprisoned by your own thoughts/a restrictive situation.

Prison warden – a person who acts as your jailer and is controlling you.

Public house – a person serving others in many different ways.

Riding stables – a person with immense spiritual power who can help you with your development.

Run down building – a person who is run down.

School – the school of life where we are continuously learning lessons/a person who schools others about life.

Semi detached house – two people attached to one and other/a part of you.

Shop – a person or situation that is serving others.

Terraced house – a person linked to others/ part of a group.

Tower – a person who is a tower of strength.

University – life and lessons that have got harder and more complex.

Warehouse – a person who is spiritually aware.

Burgundy   French connection.

Burial   A situation that is over/a person you can forget about.

Bush   We are all bushes.

Burning bush – fiery person/person with a high temperature.

Overgrown bush – a person who needs cutting down to size.

Prickly bush – prickly person.

Butchers   A meeting place.

Cafe   Person or people serving quick snack food (words)/not much substance.

Cage   A person feeling or being imprisoned/a cagey person.

Call   A wake up call/someone trying to attract your attention.

Camera   A person who can snap, and keep things from the past/putting you in the picture.

Camouflage A cover up.

Candle   To lighten your way/bring light to the situation/help you to see when you are in the dark.

Carousel   A person or situation going around and around.

Carpet   Something that is underfoot/a current situation.

Underlay – something to make the going easier.

Carrier bag A person carrying other peoples problems.

Cellar   Your lower self/the dark and negative side of you.

Cement   A bond/a grounding situation/to help with foundations.

Chains   Links/a person chained by thoughts or a situation.

Chair   A situation you are sitting on/someone is sitting on something.

Champagne A celebration.

Chandelier A group of enlightened people giving light to others.

Cherub   A precious person.

Chest   Something in front of you/get it off your chest.

Chewing gum   Something to chew over but never swallow.

Child   A person who hasn't grown/a part of you that needs to be nurtured in order to grow.

Children   A group of people who are acting childish.

Chimney   A release for an emotional situation/no smoke without fire/a warning.

Choke   Someone or something is choking you/something that is hard to swallow.

Christmas   Celebration/a new beginning for this age.

Cigar   Warning about your material life.

Cigarette   Warning about health.

Clap   An acknowledgement of something well done.

Clock   All clocks can be a situation or a person.

Alarm clock – wake up/something to be alarmed about.

Clock off – stop.

Clock on – get on with it.

Clock someone/strike someone or note something.

Cuckoo clock – a person who is in and out of where they don't belong.

104

Grandfather clock – a person who has learnt a lot about life and is able to pace themselves.

Watch - something on hand you need to watch.

Clothes   A link with a material matter.

Apron - protection for those who are in service to others/a worker for spirit.

Armour - a protection for something in front of you.

Belt - a support for the material/to keep someone or something 'up'/a powerful blow.

Bra - something in front to support and uplift.

Cardigan - a person needing or giving an extra touch of warmth.

Cloak - a cloak of secrecy/to hide or disguise something.

Clothes line - a material matter that needs to be brought out into the open/dirty washing can be hung out in the open for all to see.

Coat - our physical body.

Corset - hold things in/shape up.

Dress - something that covers you/something that needs to be addressed.

Dressing gown - something you have to wear at the end of the day. Put up with it.

Dungarees - a worker.

Fleece - something to protect you/a person who will fleece you.

Glove - something on hand to give you warmth and protection.

Jacket - the physical body.

Jumble sale - a person in a jumble and others are taking advantage of their vulnerability.

Jumper - a person jumping from one thing to another.

Kilt - a man who skirts around things.

Material - money and material goods.

Moth balls - to protect the material.

Nightdress - a woman who has to put up with a situation at the end of the day.

Overall - a protection for a person who has a lot of dirty work to do.

Petticoat – something under wraps.

Pyjamas - a situation to do with a man but at the end of the day you have to wear it or put up with it.

Raincoat - protection from an emotional situation.

Shirt - a man feeling annoyed or shirty.

Skirt - someone skirting around a situation.

Tie - a man who will have things tied up for the future.

Tie pin – a person keeping things in place for the future.

Trousers - a person in control as they are wearing the trousers.

Underwear - something personal.

Uniform - a person who has to conform.

Clover   Things are going well.

Clown   A person wearing a mask/
hiding something/someone clowning around
in life/making people laugh.

Club   People of like minds.

Coat of arms   A belief - something to aspire
too.

Coffee   Wake up/perk up. Something
 to keep you going.

Coil   A person or a situation that is
wound up.

Colour

Black – spiritual/healing.

*Black/white – seeing things in black and
white.*

Blue - the blues or depression.

Brown – the material.

Cream – the top/grandmother/a person that's been whipped.

Dark green – negativity.

Gold - highest form of wisdom.

Grey – Things are looking grey.

Light green or lime green – balanced way of thinking.

Orange - wisdom

Pink – emotionally balanced.

Purple – a spiritual connection.

Red – seeing red/emotionally imbalanced.

Silver – the highest form of spirituality.

White – balance.

Computer   We are all computers.

Computer hard drive – the mind.

Computer hardware – the physical body.

Computer mouse – the third eye.

Containers   We are all containers, our body contains our spirit.

Flask - a person who is hot and cold/a contained person.

Jar – a person who is jarring on you.

Jar of pickles – someone in a pickle.

Pepper pot – a hot tempered person.

Salt pop – a person who is all cried out.

Tin of beans – someone who is full of life.

Cook   To cook up something. How much time and what ingredients have gone in to what is being cooked ? Something that is quickly cooked has not had a lot of planning.

Cork   A positive person who is on top of life/bobbing along.

Cotton wool   A delicate person or situation.

Country lane An open pathway in life.

Countryside - a situation or person who is out in the open.

Covering   A situation that is being covered up. The type of covering would be important.

Crab   A person born in the sign of

Cancer/a person who   will cling
            on/a person
going sideways/a crabby person.

Cracker   A person being pulled in two directions.

Cradle   A new happening that is safe.

Cross   A burden you carry in life/crossroads.

Crossed swords   A situation that has been resolved/the battle is over.

Crossword   It is a puzzle but with a bit of effort you can crack it/an argument.

Crown   The   best   is   ahead/an achievement for ahead.

Crush   A   person   or   situation   at breaking point/a strong attraction.

Cry   A cry for help.

Crystal   A valuable person, a lot has gone in to shaping and polishing them/a source of energy/crystal clear.

Cup   A person who has lost a partner. They are on their own.

Cup and saucer - a couple.

Cup of tea – a person who should take a break/refresh yourself.

Curtains   Curtains are our view on life – if you have no view then the curtains are not open and you cannot see or understand life. The more they are open the more you see and understand. The colour of the curtains is important.

Curtains wide open - our view and understanding of life is immense.

Dagger   At daggers drawn/back stabber.

Dancing   Someone leading you a merry dance/in step with someone or something.

Darkness   A person who is kept in the dark/someone who has lost their way.

Darning needle   A situation where you have to make do and mend.

Dart   Get to the point.

Dartboard – something to aim for.

Dawn   Wake up to what is around you/recognise what is going on.

Deaf   Falling on deaf ears/there is a need for you to listen.

Death   Ending of something/change.

Demon   Something we have to confront, such as alcoholism/a person who torments.

Dent   Your pride has been hurt.

Desert   A person feeling desolate/life is barren.

Devil   A   mischievous   or   wicked person.

Diamond   A person of worth who has been shaped and polished.

Rough diamond – a person who needs to shape up/a person who might not be polished but is a diamond.

Dice   A person throwing caution to the wind/take a chance in life.

Dig   Dig deeper into a person or situation/having a dig.

Diploma   Well done you have passed.

Dirt   A situation or person that needs cleaning up/dishing the dirt.

Disguise   A person or situation that is not what it seems.

Disinfectant   A person who cleans up other peoples mess.

Dispensary   A person dispensing advice to make others feel better.

Divorce   A new life by divorcing yourself from something or someone

Doctor   A healer.

Doll   A female.

Barbie doll – not a lot inside/a bimbo.

China doll – a female who is fragile.

Dolls house - a female who has not grown up and is child like.

Rag doll – a female who is weary/has no backbone.

Door   A door of opportunity/way in to you/your mouth.

Closed door – difficult to get to you/ untrustworthy person/unreadable/end of a situation.

Doormat - someone who lets others step over them.

Locked doors - need the key to get this person or situation to open up.

Open door – anyone can get to you/honest person/an opening in life.

Drain — A situation that is draining you.

Drowsey — Wake up.

Dummy — A comforter/a fool.

Dungeon — Our lower self/a negative person confined by their thoughts.

Dustbin — A person with rubbish they need to get rid of/a glutton.

Earring — Within a year – two earrings within two years.

Earth — An earth mother/a person who is down to earth.

Elastic — A person or situation that can be stretched/a person that can snap.

Elbow — Give someone or something the elbow.

Emaciated — A person or situation that has no weight or influence/something or someone that is wasted.

Embryo   The start of a new beginning.

Engagement Ring   A commitment.

Engine   A power within that keeps you going.

Engineer - someone who fixes things within.

Entertainer   A person willing to please.

Envelope   A person carrying news.

Eskimo   A person who can weather cold conditions of life/a cold person.

Exam   A testing situation.

Executioner   A person putting an end to a situation.

Explorer   Someone who explores all situations to get to the bottom of things.

Explosion   Something that can blow up in your face.

Extinguisher   A person putting out emotional situations.

Eye   Keep a look out/open your eyes/third eye.

Face   Something ahead that you have to face.

Smacked face – something is smacking you in the face, trying to get your attention.

Fairy   Hairy fairy person /a delicate and spiritual person.

Fall   Heading for a fall.

Fan   Something to cool you down/ keep you cool in a situation.

Fanfare - an announcement for something positive.

Fan mail - keep cool when communicating with someone.

Fang   A person who can hurt you with their biting comments.

Farm   A collection of different types of people.

Farmer - someone sowing seeds of wisdom.

Feather   A feather in your cap, an achievement.   Well done.

Feet   Your direction in life. What is on the feet is also to do with direction.

Bare foot - no direction in life.

Big toe - a person who needs to 'toe the line' big time.

Corn - an annoying situation caused by pressure and affecting your direction in life.

Footprints - a situation that has left it's mark.

Heel - something that is behind you/bringing someone or something to heel.

Muddy feet – muddy situation, be careful.

Toe - a person who needs to 'toe the line'.

Fete   Something that comes in to your life at the right time and was meant to be.

Field   Pastures green or new.

119

File   Something that needs to be
retained.

Film   Something that can happen
again and again – being played out.

Finger   Something on hand – finger in
all things.

Fire   Emotions.

Ashes - emotions burned out.

*Camp fire – emotions out in the open/people
making trouble outside.*

Empty grate – no love there.

*Fire engine - person responding to an
emotional crisis – helping to put it out.*

Fire grate – love in the heart.

*Fire guard - stops a person falling
out/guarding emotions.*

*Fireman – a person helping to put out an
emotional situation.*

Fireplace – the focal point of the emotions.

Furnace - a person that gets red hot.

Marble fireplace – conditions are very cold.

Wooden fireplace – an emotional connection to the family.

Fish   We are all fish in the sea of life.

Aquarium - people confined in a situation.

Battered fish – someone taking a battering in life.

Dolphin – lovely person/a spiritual person.

Fish – a person born in the sign of Pisces.

Fishing rod - a person who can reel you in/someone getting hooked.

Fishmonger – a person telling a fishy tail which can cause a stink/a dubious character.

Goldfish – people in life going around and around, getting nowhere.

Jellyfish – A person who is not stable and they will sting you if you try to help.

Kipper – *a person who has been flattened/ something smells fishy.*

Octopus – *a person who can't keep their hands to themselves/many hands make light work.*

Plaice – *a person feeling flat.*

Piranha – *a person who shows no remorse and will eat you alive.*

Rainbow trout – *a colourful person.*

Salmon – *a person who survives against the odds, they have to swim against the tide.*

Shark – *a person to beware of.*

Trout –*an elderly woman regarded as being silly.*

Floor   What is underfoot or going on in your life. The colour of the floor is important.

Flowers   We are all flowers.

Blossom   A person or situation that will blossom.

Bluebell – A person with the 'blues' who is not afraid to tell others how they feel.

Bouquet – a bunch of different people.

Daffodil – a person who speaks in a positive way/a Welsh person.

Daisy - a person who always comes back up after being cut down.

Elder flower – an older person.

Freesia – a very sweet person.

Geranium - a bright and constant person.

Iris – a situation or person you should focus on.

Ivy – someone who clings to others.

Jasmine – a person with the potential to climb high but they need support.

Lavender – a person who soothes and relaxes you.

Marigold – a wise and positive female.

Orchid – a delicate person who has to be nurtured.

Plant – a person who is a spy.

Poppy - a November symbol/remembrance.

Red rose – pure love.

Rose – a loving person, they have a heart.

Rosebush – a person who is quite prickly but has a lot of heart.

Snowdrop – a balanced person who has come through the cold times but has remained sweet of nature.

Sunflower – a person standing out from the crowd, as they are such a positive and sunny personality.

Tulip – Your mouth and what you say - two lips.

Violet – a shy woman/a shrinking violet.

Wallflower - an observer in life/a person who is always overlooked.

Water lily – A woman able to keep afloat in life.

White rose – thank you.

Yellow rose – thank you for being positive.

Food   Spiritual substance/food for thought.

Apple pie - knowledge that is served to you in an enjoyable way.

Bacon - saving someone or something in a situation.

Beans - someone full of beans.

Biscuit - that takes the biscuit/the final thing.

Box of chocolates - people who are individuals.

Bread - spiritual knowledge.

Breakfast - something that can set you up for the day. Full breakfast, a lot on your plate

Butter – aunty/buttering someone up.

Cake - a lot of preparation has gone in to a cake/a recipe.

Cheese – father.

Cheesecake – a father figure that gives a good foundation.

Chips - someone who will be given their marching orders as they have had their chips.

Chocolate - Something nice to share with others.

Corned beef - a male person who is contained – you will need the key to open and understand him.

Cottage cheese – father who is too soft.

Cream – grandmother.

Egg - a new beginning/an idea or situation about to hatch.

Fried egg – a person always showing their sunny side/see the sunny side of a situation.

Gravy – an unexpected piece of good luck.

Honey - feeds within, a lot goes into honey.

Ice cream - a problem that has to be licked in life but the outcome is satisfying.

Jelly - an unstable person or situation.

Lollipop - a problem that you can lick.

Marshmallow - A person who is too soft.

Meat - something to chew over.

Pancake – a person or situation that is as flat as a pancake.

Picnic - something out in the open giving food for thought/an easy task.

Raw sausage – a person who is still hurting.

Rice – a new start in life.

Rice pudding – a new start in life that will not be so hard.

Saccharine - a person who pretends to be sweet but they are not genuine.

Sauce – a cheeky person.

Sausage – a person, we are all in a skin.

Stew – a person in a stew or a mess.

Sugar – sugar and sweets feed the psychic.

Syrup - a sticky situation.

Toast – words of congratulations for something that has been achieved.

Trifle – a trifling problem that has been built up out of all proportion.

Tripe – someone is talking a load of old tripe or rubbish.

Fool   A person who does not take life seriously.

Fossil   A spiritual person – someone who is valuable.

Frisbee   Something that comes back to you but is not of much value.

Frog   A person with very little concentration. They hop from one thing to another.

Front   The future - something before
us.

Frown   Disapproval   for   something
ahead.

Fruit and Vegetables

Apple - a teacher/someone who wants to share the fruits of their wisdom.

Avocado - a bland and negative person.

Banana – something positive, hold on for too long and it will go bad/good intentions falling by the wayside.

Beetroot - an embarrassing situation/not in control of emotions.

Broccoli – a negative person.

Cabbage - someone that does not absorb a lot.

Carrot – something to keep you going forward.

Cauliflower – a person who won't listen as they have cauliflower ears.

Celery – a straight, no-nonsense person who is crisp and to the point.

Cherry – a person who appears soft but has a hard inside/cherry on the top.

Coconut - a hard nut to crack.

Corn - a seed you have planted and grown, and bears fruit.

Cucumber – A negative person who has no substance.

Damson - a tiny female but with so much within/damsel in distress.

Gooseberry – a thick skinned person.

Grape – enriches your life/turns water into wine.

Grapevine - a group of people who work to enrich others lives.

Leak – A person who gives a lot to others but can become drained because of this/a Welsh person.

Lemon – a person who had been taken advantage of/a bitter person.

Mushroom – a person in the dark/a person who has grown despite being in the dark.

Nut - a crazy or eccentric person/a person who is hard to crack.

Nutcracker - a person who can crack the hardest problem.

Onion – a person who has many layers to their emotions.

Orange – knowledge from the tree of wisdom. You have to peel it to get to the wisdom, a piece at a time.

Peach – teach/a teacher.

Peas – like minded people – two peas in a pod.

Pickle – a person or situation that is in a mess.

Pineapple – prickly and thick skinned person.

Pip – an annoying person.

Potato – someone who sits around doing nothing – a couch potato.

Prune – an ill tempered and stupid person.

Radish – A person who gets hot under the collar easily.

Red apple – teacher that is not in control.

Rhubarb – someone talking a load of rhubarb/sharp words.

Strawberry – a heart that is easily crushed.

Sweet corn – a positive and young person who enjoys being in service with others.

Tomato - a woman, 'gorgeous tomato'.

Frying pan Going from one emotional situation to the other/a person or situation that might overheat.

Fugitive Someone hiding from life or themselves.

Funeral A gathering of people burying a situation so that they can lay it to rest.

Coffin - nailing something down and putting it to rest.

Grave – a serious situation laid to rest.

Mourners – people who are mourning the loss of something or someone.

Undertaker - a person who will take the burden of ending a situation and putting it to rest.

Funfair   An affair that is fun.

Funfair ride – enjoying the thrill of the ride.

Fungus   A situation or person that is rotten.

Fur   A person with an added warmth.

Furniture   Situations and thoughts.

Gaffer   A person in control of others and giving the orders.

Gag   A person or situation that has been silenced/restrain yourself.

Gallery   A colourful person who can put you in the picture about so many things in life.

Gambler   Someone who takes a chance or gamble.

Garage   A place of safety to park yourself for a rest/a person working to repair others.

Garden   What you put in to life.

Back garden – the past.

Empty garden – you've put nothing in your life.

Fence - a feeling of being fenced in/a boundary/to pass on something that doesn't belong to you.

Front garden – the future.

Full garden – full life.

Gardener – A person putting a lot of effort into life/ you reap what you sow.

Garden fork - dig over something, break it down with a lot of effort.

Garden gate -　　　　your mouth.

Garden path – your direction in life.

Garden shears - something on hand to keep things in trim/cut back on something in life.

Grass - something afoot that needs to be kept under control/grass is greener on the other side.

Greenhouse – a person tenderly helping others to grow/a person who should not throw stones.

Hedge – To be hedged in/hedge your bets.

Hole - a person in a hole - digging a hole for themselves.

Landscape - your outlook on life.

Lawn - a situation or person who needs constant care to keep in shape.

Lawn mower - help on hand to keep what is underfoot in shape.

*Mud - slanderous or defamatory comments –
mud sticks/a person who has muddied the
water so that emotions are clouded.*

Neat garden – life in order.

*Overgrown garden – your life needs sorting
out.*

Prune – a need to cut back.

*Rake – to rake over the coals of a hot
situation/a man who is immoral/rake in the
benefits.*

*Scythe - a person reaping what they have
sown.*

*Seed – the planting of something for growth
and development/seed of an idea.*

*Shed – a person who is a loner or alone in
life, but they hold all the tools to put life (the
garden) in order.*

*Spade - spade work/ groundwork. A lot to do
to get it right/digging over something.*

*Trowel – to lay something on thick –
exaggerate something.*

Weed – a person who needs to be weeded or taken out of your life.

Garter   An added support.

Gas   Gassing about something –
poison.

Gem   A person of value.

General   A leader – someone who helps
with life's battles.

Gentry   Someone who feels he is above
others.

Ghetto   A situation from which it is
difficult to escape.

Ghost   Someone from the past.

Giant   Someone who has large
spiritual growth.

Gift   Someone or something to be
thankful for.

Girder   A person shouldering
responsibility/holding others up.

Gladiator   A person who is prepared to fight in life.

Glass   A fragile person/something or someone you can see through.

Glasses - spectacles.   Help in seeing things

more clearly.

Brown glasses – material needs to be looked at.

New glasses – change your view on life.

Reading glasses – to help you read into the situation.

Rose tinted glasses – an unrealistic view.

Sun glasses - can help or hinder our view.

Glue   A situation you are stuck with/a person sticking like glue.

Glutton   Someone never learning from their mistakes – a glutton for punishment.

Gnome   A male stuck in a rut in life.

Governor   Someone who is in control of others.

Grease   Something or someone that could make you slip/grease someone's palm.

Grill   A situation where questions need to be asked.

Guard   Something for protection.

Guardian   Someone who takes responsibility for your wellbeing/someone helping you to grow.

Guillotine   Severing something for ahead.

Gun   Someone is gunning for you.

Gutter   A situation where you have felt at your lowest.

Gymnasium   A person limbering up in preparation for life's trials.

Gypsy   A restless person.

Haberdashery   Someone concerned with the little things in life that help to keep things together.

Hair   Something for ahead.

Bald - nothing there for ahead.

Blonde - someone who will be enlightened ahead.

Comb - something for ahead to get rid of the tangles and put things in order.

Curly hair– twists and turns ahead.

Fringe – a situation in front of you that is going to be cut short/there is a need to cut something short.

Hairband - people securing something for ahead.

Hairclip - securing something for ahead.

Haircut – something being cut back or reshaped for ahead.

Hairdresser - seeing to things for ahead/styling and shaping for the future.

Hairdressing scissors - cut into shape for ahead.

Hairnet - keeping things just right for ahead, nothing will be out of place.

Lacquer   To secure something for ahead.

Long and straight hair – straight ahead/lasting a long time.

Pulled back hair – a situation is behind you.

Ribbon – Tying up something for ahead.

Short hair – short cut ahead.

Wig – something for ahead which is not real or something or someone covering up for ahead.

Hall   The passage of time.

Halo   The aura/light ahead to help you through the darkness.

Hand   Something on hand/in hand/a person giving a helping hand.

Cold hands – warm heart.

141

Knarled hands – a knotted situation that is in hand and under control.

Handbag   Something personal to be kept to yourself/a personal situation.

Hand basin   Surface problem to be dealt with.

Handcuffs   Your hands are tied.

Handkerchief
Something in hand to help with an emotional situation.

Harness   To take control.

Harpoon   Someone who can hurt when making a point.

Harvest   The result of what you sow in life.

Hatch   An idea about to be born.

Hats   Something for ahead 'on ahead'. Different hats, different situations. If a hat were in your hand – it's all in hand.

Bathing hat - something close for ahead that will offer you protection in life.

Beret – one sided situation ahead.

Cap – keeping something to yourself and under your cap.

Graduation hat – you have learned lessons in life and have graduated

with flying colours.

Helmet – protection for ahead.

Miners hat –a powerful protection for ahead.

Policeman's helmet – a dependable force for ahead.

Scarf – keeping things in place for ahead.

Skullcap – something that is close ahead.

Sun hat – protection from heated words.

Yodellers hat – something ahead you would have to use your voice for.

Headlines   Something that attracts your attention.

Headmaster Someone who has mastered things in life and is an example to others.

Heart   An emotional situation/don't let your heart rule your head.

Heaven   A happy state of mind – heaven on earth.

Hell   A negative state of mind.

Hermit   A loner.

Highwayman
A person who takes what they want.

Hitchhiker   A person always looking for a free ride.

Hook   Caught up in a situation – being hooked in.

Hoop   A situation all around you – step out of it.

Hopscotch   A skill you can learn by keeping on your toes.

Horn   Horn of plenty.

Hot water bottle   Someone who gives warmth and comfort/someone who gives comfort.

Humble pie   Someone who is wrong and needs to admit it.

Humpty Dumpty   Someone set for a fall and will need a pick-me-up.

Hurdle   An obstacle to overcome.

Hypnotist   A person who likes to control others.

Ice cube   A person able to cool and calm a situation.

Icon   A person of status.

Identity bracelet   Something you need to keep on hand to remind you of who you are.

Idol   Someone who is worshipped, but be careful they are not a false God.

145

Igloo   A person who has an inner warmth but appears cold on the outside.

Imitation   Someone or something that is not the real thing/a person lacking self confidence who imitates others.

Imp   A loveable but mischievous person.

Incinerator   Someone who can reduce your hopes and dreams to ashes.

Indenture   An agreement between two people for the unforeseeable future.

Indicator   An indication of which direction you should take.

Infant   A childish person/the spiritual part of you that needs to be nurtured in order to grow.

Inflammation An emotional situation that has flared up.

Injection   A person or situation needing input to improve matters.

Ink   Communication that can't be taken back.

Ink well   People dipping in to your resources but be careful as they might leave a mark.

Insects   We are all insects.

Ants - people who are industrious and are team workers.

Bee - someone who feeds you something sweet/a psychic person/a busy person/a worker.

Bug - a situation or person that is bugging you/a spy.

Butterfly - transition from one life to another. A person who has shed their earthly body.

Caterpillar - a period of transformation/a person who is struggling to be free.

Flea – a person who will suck your blood – go from one to the other.

Fly - an irritating person/fly on the wall (spy)/take flight/a flirtatious person.

Grub - a grubby situation or person.

Hive - a lot going on – a hive of activity.

Maggot - a person or a situation that is eating away at you.

Nits - someone who is infested by unpleasant thoughts/feeling lousy/a person who nit picks.

Slug - a slimy person.

Spider – a person who will weave a web to trap you 'oh what a tangled web we weave when trying to deceive'.

Wasp – a person with a sting.

Worm - person who tries to worm out of something.

The worm turns/bait – take the bait.

Intruder   An intrusive person or situation.

Invasion   An invasion of privacy.

Iron   A person or situation that needs to be ironed out.

Ironing board - a support to help smooth out problems.

Island   A person who is isolated.

Jackpot   A gamble that has paid off.

Jade   A person feeling jaded and under the weather.

Jail   Locking away feelings and emotions/confining someone or something.
Jaundiced   A person with a tainted view on life.

Jaw   A person who likes to talk.

Locked jaw – a person locked in a verbal battle.

Jester   A person making exaggerated gestures that can fool you.

Jet spray   Pressures of life.

Jewel   A person or situation of immense value.

Jigsaw   A puzzle in life that can be worked out with a little effort.

Jockey   A person who can handle power.

Jog   A person or situation that is jogging along.

Journey   Our life is a journey we should learn from in order to grow. We should enjoy that journey without focusing too much on the destination.

Judge   A person who is a good judge of character/a judgemental person.

Junction   A choice of direction in life.

Jury   A group of people with the power to effect a person or situation.

Kaleidoscope   A very changeable but colourful person.

Kettle   A person quick to come to the boil and let off steam.

Key   An opportunity in life to unlock something.

King   A king amongst men/a person born in the sign of Leo.

150

Kiss   Sealed with a kiss – a seal of approval.

Kissing - paying lip service.

Kitchen   Where you prepare to serve spirit/mankind. The quality of what you serve depends on the effort you have put in to the preparation.

Kite   A high flier – something that is taking off. Whose pulling the strings?

Knave   A male who is untrustworthy as he has not grown emotionally.

Knee   A need to bend a little – be more flexible.

Knees - you could be brought to your knees.

Knife   A situation or person who can cause you a stab of pain/to cut through a situation and break things down for ease of understanding.

Fork - holding back by securing words.

Knife and fork – Something on hand to help you understand the words that have been spoken, or to understand life. Cut up, chew over and swallow what you can, and spit out what you can't.

Knight   A man who will come to your rescue when you are at your darkest hour.

Knitting needles Something on hand to bring together a pattern or plan.

Wooden knitting needles – a plan in hand to bring the family together.

Knock   Someone trying to get your attention so you can let them in/something having a knock on effect.

Knot   A problem that needs to be untied or tied up.

Label   A situation or person that needs to be made clear/a judgemental person.

Laboratory   A person who will investigate to find the answers/a situation that needs researching to get to the bottom of it.

Ladders   An opportunity to better one's self.

Lamp   A person who can bring light to the situation.

Lampshade   A protection for someone who is giving too much of themselves.

Lane   A pathway in life – a way out of a situation but keep your wits about you .

Larder   Somewhere that food is stored – spiritual food.

Late   A person or situation that is not on time or is delayed/a deceased person.

Leap   Look before you leap/a leap of faith.

Leather   A tough person who wears well.

Seasoned leather – a person who has lots of life experience and is tough because of it.

Ledger   A person trying to get the balance in life right – something doesn't add up.

Lego   Building something/pick up the pieces/put the pieces together.

Legs   A support for life.

Letter   A Communication.

Level   A situation where someone needs to level with you.

Lick   A problem which needs to be overcome.

Lid   Keep the lid on something.

Lift   A person giving others a lift when they are down.

Light   A person bringing light to the situation to help you to see/someone providing light relief.

Flashing lights - a means of getting your attention.

Link   A tie or a bond. Something connecting people or situations.

Lips   A lippy person.

Litter   A lot of rubbish being spread around about someone or something.

Rubbish - a person or situation.

Lock   The means of securing something.

Locket   Something personal and close to your heart.

Loft   Our subconscious mind.

Lollipop Lady   A female watching out for others and helping them in life.

Lost   Unable to find your way in life/a person or situation that is beyond reach.

Luggage   A weight you carry from your past.

Magician   A person who can make things happen.

Magnet   A person who draws others to them.

Magnifying glass   A person who is very particular and examines every detail/a person who magnifies and exaggerates.

Mangle   A person who has been through the mangle – they are emotionally wrung out.

Manuscript – something on hand where what has been said is important.

Map   Something in life is mapped out for you but you can change direction and find another way to get there.

Marbles   Someone not in control.

Market   A chaotic situation/lots of choices in life but make sure you choose what is of value.

Market stall – something you are being asked to 'buy' or accept.

Marquee   An added protection for a situation/a place of shelter for a short while .

Mascot   A person bringing good luck for an event in life.

Mask   A person wearing a mask to hide their true feelings.

Match   A situation or person that can easily ignite.

Maze   Confusing and interconnecting pathways in life – you have to find your way out of a situation.

Meadow   Pastures green – pastures new.

Meal   Food for thought.

Media   A person or situation offering the means to communicate something out loud.

Medicine   A person with the remedy for health or problems/someone having a taste of their own medicine.

Meditation   A means of contemplation.

Mermaid   A woman of great beauty and charm who can lure you into an emotionally vulnerable situation.

Midwife   A woman assisting in the beginning of something.

Milk   A mother or mother figure who will provide everything that is needed to help you to grow.

Glass of milk – motherly instincts becoming clear.

Milk churn – motherly emotions all churned up.

Spilt milk - do not cry over spilt milk.

Teat – to milk someone dry.

Mirror   Take a good look at yourself and reflect– mirror image.

Money   Power, as it is a currency (current).

Bank - a power source, where the currency builds up and is stored.

Banker – a powerful person who can empower you.

Cheque - something needs to be checked.

Coins – a spiritual power.

Fortune - a wealth of wisdom/a person seeking knowledge.

Money - power in the form of wisdom, the wiser the person the more powerful they become.

Paper money – less powerful because it doesn't last.

Penny - something that has just dawned on you – the penny has dropped/a power – currency.

Monster   Something or someone that is out of control – a monster of our own creation.

Moon   A person controlling our emotions/a moody person/a person who brings light when we are in the dark.

Mop   Cleaning up an emotional situation – mop away the tears.

Mother   Nurturing person/the nurturing side of us/the person who is working with you from spirit, helping you to grow.

Mould   A situation that has been left too long, it is decaying.

Mountain   A big problem that has to be overcome.

Alps - a mountain for you to climb but even when you get to the top, conditions will still be difficult.

Cliff - a warning not to go any further.

Cliff edge - turn back now.

Hill - a small problem.

Peak - an intense situation/reaching the top of a problem you have had to climb.

Valley - a low period in your life.

Moustache   Something under your nose but you can't see it

Move   Someone or something is on the move.

Mug   Someone who has been made a fool of.

Mummy   A situation that has been preserved but is under wraps.

Murder   A volatile situation.

Music   We all make music. It is to do with the rhythm, harmony and pace of life. Some of us go solo and others of us harmonise. Others are out of tune and there are those who are so, so sweet.

Musical Instruments   We are all instruments.

Accordion - a person who doesn't stop for breath, it is in their hands.

Bagpipes – a person who is full of wind.

Banjo - a person that makes others feel good.

Cello – a grounded person, their feet are firmly on the ground.

Clarinet – a mellow person.

Drum - a person that likes to be heard/a person who sets the pace in relationships with others.

Fiddle - don't trust a fiddle/a person on the fiddle.

Flute - a person who is gentle and sweet.

Guitar - someone who just strums along in life.

Harmonica – A person who is a mouthpiece and will speak up for others.

Harp – A person harping on/a gentle and soothing person.

Jazz - a person or situation that needs jazzing up.

Piano – a person who is in perfect harmony.

Squeeze box – a person who has been emotionally squeezed in life.

Trumpet – a person who is boastful and blows their own trumpet.

Violin – a person tugging at your heart strings.

Muzzle   A person who needs to restrain their words, think before you speak.

Naked   A person or situation that is, or will be, exposed.

Nausea   A person or situation that makes you feel sick.

Neck   A support for something that is ahead of you.

Choker   A person or situation that is choking you.

Necklace   Links with a person or situation who will support you for ahead.

Needle   Someone or something that is needling you.

Neglect   A person or situation that is in need of love and care.

Neighbour   A part of you and your personality/someone who is close to you/ someone you are attached too.

Net   A safety net/a situation you are caught up in.

Newsagent   A giver of information, but this person could also be a scandal monger.

Night   You are in the dark about something or someone.

Nod   Someone in agreement with you and is giving you the nod.

Nomad   A person who can't settle at anything – they are constantly on the move.

Nose   A nosey person/a smell to alert you.

Flared nostrils – an angry person.

Nudge   A person given a nudge to wake them up to a situation.

Nurse   A carer or healer, nursing people through their problems.

Nursemaid   Someone with enough patience to help people, even though their behaviour is childlike.

Nursery   A person who fosters and develops new beginnings.

Oil   A person who can inflame or calm.

Pouring oil – pouring oil over troubled waters to inflame the situation.

Ointment   Something on hand to bring relief to a person or situation.

Opening   A door of opportunity opening up for you.

Outlaw   An habitual criminal/a rebel who will not conform.

Oyster   A person who is hard to get into but when you do you find they have wisdom, a pearl of wisdom.

Pearl - a person who has been through many, many life experiences to gain wisdom.

Pearl necklace – wisdom that will support you for ahead.

Pace   Pace yourself.

Paint   Something to brighten or freshen your life/to gloss over something.

Undercoat – preparation to be done before you can proceed.

Pantomime   Communication by way of gesture and facial expression - a person who exaggerates.

Paper   To paper over the cracks – a flimsy solution that can easily be torn apart.

Parliament   A decision that will govern your life.

Party   Something to celebrate/be party to something.

Passageway The passage of time.

Passenger   Someone or something you are taking along with you in life.

Patch   A person or a situation that has been repaired – patch things up.

Path   The path trodden in life.

Pattern   A repetitive pattern of behaviour, a person having to look at their faults/a template for life that can be used again and again.

Pavement   A safe path to follow in life.

Pawn   A person who has been used.

Pawnbroker - a person wanting interest or pay-back for their help in redeeming a situation.

Pay   A price to pay/reward/pay-back like karma.

Pebbles   People in your life, often from the past, as they are connected to sands of time.

Pedestrian   A person going forward in life at their own pace and under their own steam.

Pedestrian bridge – a faster route/ a means of bridging a gap to help you to be where you are supposed to be.

Peg   A means of securing a material problem.

Pen   A person or situation that needs expression/communication.

Pencil   A person or situation that is changeable.

167

Perfume   The very essence of a person.

Picture   Putting you in the picture, or letting you know about something.

Pillar   A support/a well respected person.

Pimple   An eruption of emotions.

Pin   Securing the material.

Pioneer   A brave person not afraid to tackle new experiences.

Pipe   Warning about your mouth - be careful what you say.

Water pipe – problem with your Plumbing/ emotional outlet.

White pipe – peace.

Pistol   An explosive situation in your hands.

Pit   Our lower self/our fears.

Planet   A person or situation which is out of reach.

Plastic   A person or situation that is a fake.

Plate   Something that is served to you.

Plate full - a lot going on in your life.

Platform   An opportunity to express yourself.

Poker   A person or situation that has been stirred up emotionally.

Pole   Something on hand to elevate you/a support.

Policeman   A person who will look out for you and keep you safe.

Polish   A person or situation that needs careful attention in their presentation.

Porter   A person who carries other peoples load.

Powder puff   Something on hand to provide the finishing touches for something you have to face.

Power point   A person or situation who is a source of extra strength.

Plug - a person wasting energy on others.

Pram   Pushing ahead with a new beginning or idea.

Pregnant   Something you are passionate about and carry around with you as it is your 'baby'/an expectation of a new happening.

Prescription   A remedy that is in hand to help you to heal.

Puppet   A person who is controlled by others and lets them pull the strings.

Purse   A person or a situation that is very personal.

Empty purse – a person or situation of little value.

Full purse – a person or situation of value.

Purse strings - someone having financial control over you/someone in control as they have the power.

Puzzle   A person or situation that is baffling, but with a bit of effort the pieces will come together.

Pyramid   A person or a situation that has been laid to rest but there is a point to it.

Quarry   A stony situation where you need to dig deep to find strength/to pursue someone.

Quartz   A person who is a rock and of great value.

Queen   A woman who rules the roost.

Quest   To search for something or someone.

Question   A person searching for answers.

Queue   A need for patience in a situation but eventually you will have your turn.

Quicksand   A situation where in time you will realise you are not on solid ground.

Quintuplets   Representing the five senses.

171

Raffle ticket   A person who takes a gamble in life.

Ransom – a person being held for ransom. A price to pay to resolve the situation.

Rape   Abusive or improper treatment - a violation against someone or something.

Rash   A decision made in haste/an outbreak of many instances within a brief period.

Razor blade – a sharp person/something to smooth over what is facing you.

Record   A person playing the same old tune.

Reflection   Something you have to face up to/reflect on a situation.

Rigid   A person who needs to bend a little.

Rock   A person offering strong support.

Stick of rock – a sticky situation.

172

Rocking horse
A person going nowhere.

Roller skates Put your skates on and get
going.

Rooms   Different facets of our
personality.

Rubber   Rub out something or
someone from your life.

Run   A person who needs to run
away from a situation.

*Chase – pursuing a situation or a
person.*

Sack   A situation or person who is no
longer needed/a bed, mattress or sleeping
bag.

Safe   A person who should keep their
combination safe and not allow others to get
to them.

Salute   A tribute for something you
have achieved in the battle of life.

Scar   An emotional situation that is visible/a person carrying a scar.

Scissors   Cut - stop.

Scorpion   A person who will sting you with their words. A person born in the sign of Scorpio.

Seesaw   A situation between two people who are up one minute and down the next.

Settee   A situation that people are sitting on.

Two seater settee – two people are sitting on a situation.

Sewing machine
Bringing your material life together.

Sex   Something very personal between two people.

Person on top – someone or something getting the better of you, or getting on top of you in a private and personal situation.

Shave   Smoothing problems that are facing you/a close shave.

Shelf   A situation or a person that has been put to one side and is on the shelf.

Shelf life - a person or situation that needs to be shelved.

Shell   A dead person or situation.

Sherry   A person who has been fortified or made strong.

Shield   Something or someone to protect you.

Shoes   To do with your direction

Ballet shoes – stay on your toes.

Darned socks – a person who has had to make do and mend in their material life.

Laces – To tighten things securely for the direction you take.

Sandals – your direction in life is opening up/opportunities opening up for you.

Slippers – a rest from the situation.

Socks - extra protection for your direction.

Stout shoes – a durable person.

Tap shoes – somebody who is on tap or available when needed.

Trainers – a person in training or in need of training.

Wellingtons – complete protection.

Workman's shoes – work for you.

Sideboard   Something very personal that no one should be allowed to delve into.

Sister   A female who is like a sister to you/could be a part of your personality.

Skull   The support for whatever is ahead.

Slab   To help bury something/something of substance or weight.

Slave   A person who is a slave to others, or is enslaved by their own thoughts.

Slide   Someone passing smoothly over a slippery situation/let the matter slide.

Smell   A sensing that should tell you something.

Bad smell – something doesn't smell right.

Sweet smell – sweet smell of success.

Smoke   A hazard warning.

Smoke alarm - a health warning, don't delay in taking action.

Soap   A situation that is like a soap opera.

Soldier – someone who has to soldier on/a person with a fighting spirit.

Solicitor   A legal person or situation – someone or something that can represent or help you.

Soot   The residue of an emotional time.

Spice   Spice up your life.

Spinning top Someone who is in a spin.

Spout   A person who is spouting off about something.

Staircase   Rise above it/take your thoughts up gradually, step by step.

Statue – a person who is unmovable and cold.

Steel   Someone hard enough to take the knocks in life.

Sticky   A sticky situation.

Sticky mud – mud sticks.

Sting   A painful situation which has a point to it/a person cheating.

String   A person being strung along/a situation that could go on and on 'how long is a piece of string?'.

Stop   Don't go

any further.

Suit   A person or situation that is to do with business.

Sun   A person that gives out a lot of love and warmth/a much loved son.

Swing   A person or situation getting nowhere/going back and forth with a problem.

Table   Where you serve – helping others.

Coffee table – aim to raise your service a little higher.

Wooden table – serving the family.

Tail   A situation or tale you should place behind you.

Tattoo   A person or situation that has left its mark on you.

Tax   A penalty - a taxing situation/pay back.

Tea   Rest – refresh yourself/take a break.

Teacher   A person who has learned about life and can teach you from their own experience.

Team   Like minded people working together.

Teapot   A person that spouts out/needs to speak about something.

Teddy bear   Something from your past you cling on to.

Teeth   Words – chew things over or get your teeth into something.

False teeth – get a grip on what is being said as the words are false.

Pulling out teeth – someone is pulling the words out of your mouth.

Teeth cleaning – something spoken needs to be cleaned up.

Teeth falling out – words falling out of your mouth.

Tooth brush – a person who needs to brush up on how they speak.

Tooth paste – a person who leaves a nice taste in your mouth because of what they have said.

Telephone   Communication.

Telephone kiosk – a person who communicates well with others.

Television   A transmitter and receiver of information/a person who passes on what they have heard.

Tent   A person in a temporary situation.

Thimble   Protection for something on hand.

Throat   Control of what you say.

Hands around the throat – a person or situation that is choking you.

Red scarf around the throat – control yourself when speaking.

Toilet   Relieve yourself/pass a motion.

Tools   An advantage in any

situation – tools on   hand to fix things.

Drill – a person who can be a bore, they go on and on.

Hammer - knocking something in to shape/securing something/hammering something home.

Hatchet - a situation that needs to be buried/a person brought in to make tough decisions .

Nail - a secure person or situation/the need to nail something or someone.

Saw - something or someone that can cut problems down to size.

Scaffolding - a situation or person needing support.

Screw - a person who turns the screw to be hurtful/a person who is all screwed up inside.

Spanner - a person who could put a spanner in the works/a person who is on hand to help loosen or tighten up a situation.

Spirit level – a spiritual person whose way of thinking is balanced.

Wrench - a break or parting that causes an emotional wrench.

Torch   A person carrying a torch for someone/something in hand to light your way.

Towel   Something in hand to dry away emotions/throw in the towel.

Track   A person or situation that is on track.

Traffic lights Something that regulates our progress along our pathway of life.

Traffic Warden -need to move on, it will cost you to stay in that situation.

Tray   Something being served to you.

Silver tray – something being served to you with the highest motive.

Treasure   A person of great value/someone or something to treasure.

Treasure hunt – hunting to find the value of someone or something.

Trees   Family – roots. Anything to do with wood is linked to the family.

Acorn - the potential for growth/will grow strong.

Branch – a branch of the family.

Forest – The family/can't see the wood for the trees in a family situation.

Holly - a person who is difficult to handle.

Laurel wreath – an achievement for ahead.

Leaf – a member of the family.

184

Log – a person cut off from the family.

Pine cone – a person who has dropped out of the family and is pining.

Twig – a young member of the family.

Tunnel   A dark period we have to go through to come out the other side.

Tunnel of light
There is light at the end of the tunnel.

Twins – two people who are inseparable or alike/a duplicate situation.. A person born in the sign of Gemini.

Typewriter   Words at your fingertips.

Umberella   Shelter from the storms of life.

Union   Bringing together people or a situation/people working together for the same cause.

Vacation   A need to rest for a while.

Vaccine   A prevention for a situation that is around you.

Vanguard   Someone who is preparing the way for others to follow.

Vehicle   Our body is a vehicle that holds our spirit.

Ambulance - a person who responds to an emergency/a healer.

Bike - A person that is pushing ahead on their own effort – well balanced.

Bus - busy person who is always taking others on board, helping them to get to where they are supposed to be.

Car – we are all cars. Who is in the driving seat?

Caravan – a person always on the move and who never settles in one place.

Car-jack – A support to keep you up in your ime of need.

Car park – to stay in a situation for a period of time/a place of safety.

Coach – a teacher, coaching others.

Convertible car – a person who is too open/vulnerable.

Flat tyre – a person feeling flat because they are not getting anywhere.

Go cart - someone that has to be pushed in life.

Hearse - taking something away/laying something to rest.

Juggernaut – a person carrying a heavy load.

Limousine – a very accommodating person, larger than life who makes others feel comfortable.

Lorry - a worker.

Mechanic – a healer.

Motorbike - a power you need to know how to handle/need to be balanced to control this power.

Patrol car – an alert and caring person who protects others.

Pick-up van – a person who is flirty and is trying to 'pick you up'/a person who will pick you up when you are broken.

Racing car – a person who races through life and is always in a hurry.

Racing rally – people rushing to rally around to help in a situation.

Removal van – something or someone is now on the move.

Rolls Royce – the best.

Tricycle – a person pushing ahead by their own efforts but has extra support to keep them well balanced.

Tyre – Something to support you or help you on life's journey.

Veil   To conceal or disguise/a woman taking vows.

Velvet   A material situation that will be smoothed out.

Virgin   A pure, uncorrupted person/ an unexplored situation/a person born in the sign of Virgo.

Volcano   An emotional eruption with damaging results.

Walking stick
Support for a situation.

Wall   A difficult situation where you are 'up against the wall'/a wall of silence/ something stopping you going any further.

Wand   Something in hand to grant your wishes.

War   Trouble between people/a troublesome situation.

Washing   Preparation for something/ cleaning up a material problem.

Flannel - a person that talks a lot of flannel.

Washbasin – A surface problem to be dealt with.

Washing dirty washing – airing your business/speaking of personal matters and bringing them out in the open/cleaning up a material problem.

Washing machine – a person feeling washed out and always in a spin.

Water   Water is life - you can feel as though you are going to drown.

Calm seas – calm life.

Diver – someone who dives in to life head first.

Dock - a person on trial/a place to rest in the sea of life.

Drop anchor – stay put/high waves sweeping over you – engulfed by emotion.

Drowning - someone who is out of their depth in a situation.

Flood - uncontrollable and overwhelming emotions/floods of tears.

Glacier - a cold person who is very set in their way of thinking.

Harbour - a place of safety/a person harbouring emotions.

Lake - not a lot of movement in life, things could become stagnant.

Leaking tap – your private life is being made public.

Oasis - someone offering shelter - a place of safety or sanctuary.

Ocean- the sea of life/a deep person who you can never get to the bottom of.

Overflow - a person who has an excess of emotions.

Pier – the opportunity to view life.

Pond - life is stagnant.

Port - a safe place in a storm.

Puddle - a puddle of tears.

River – a restricted life will now open up.

Sea – sea of life.

Stormy seas – stormy life.

Swimming pool – a pool of like minded people.

Tap – how your life is running is in your

hands.

Thunder - a person making a lot of noise/a person showing disapproval with a face like thunder.

Walking on water – on top of life.

Waterfall – an emotionally turbulent situation where things have got out of hand.

Watering can – someone who helps others to grow/a refreshing person.

Water carrier – a person carrying a lot of emotion/a person born in the sign of Aquarius.

Waves – a disturbance in life as someone is making waves.

Well – deep emotions/feelings/deep person.

Whirlpool – great confusion with things going around and around in your head, sucking you down and down.

Weather   Conditions around a person or situation.

Calm weather conditions – life is calm.

Clouds - a problem in life/something overshadowing you/every cloud has a silver lining.

Cold weather - an unfriendly feeling or situation.

Fog - can't see ahead or within.

Gale - a person or situation that can cause havoc before it blows itself out.

Hailstones - a temporary situation where emotions are as cold as ice.

Hot weather – a situation that could burn you.

Hurricane - a forceful person who causes chaos.

Ice - a dangerous and emotional situation that could make you slip.

Iceberg - a cold and unfeeling person who does not show the depth of their thoughts or feelings.

Lightning - a reality that strikes you like lightening, giving clarity of thought.

Mist - a haze before the eyes that restricts what you see- a person in a haze.

Rain - tears raining down.

Rainbow - after the storm of tears comes a rainbow with a pot of gold or wisdom.

Shower of rain – tears that are soon dried up.

Snow - danger – treacherous under foot

Snow ball – cold words thrown at someone.

Stormy weather conditions – life is stormy.

Stormy weather with a tea cup involved - storm in a teacup.

Warm weather – a comfortable situation.

Wind – a force or power.

Windmill – a person who has harnessed the spiritual power to help those who are going through the mill/a person with the ability to sort the wheat from the chaff.

Winter – cold and harsh conditions.

Wedding   A new way of life.

Weighing scales   A person born in the sign of Libra/balancing the situation or weighing things up.

Wheel   What goes around comes around.

Window   Our view on life.

Narrow window – a narrow view on life.

Open window – an open view on life.

Picture window – seeing the full picture.

Round window – a well rounded view of life.

Wine   An enriched life – turning water into wine.

Wings   A person who will lift you up
and help you to rise above your problems.

Worker   An industrious person/a worker
for spirit.

Wringer   A person who has been through
the wringer in an emotional situation.

Writing   Communication.

Yarn   A person who exaggerates but
tells a good story.

Yeast   Someone who will rise
to the occasion.

Zimmer frame
A support for a fragile person.

Zip   Keep your mouth shut and
zipped.

Zombie   A person who is emotionally
dead.